BETTER *than a* CURE

One Man's Journey to Free the World of Polio

Ramesh Ferris

with

John Firth

*Thank-you for supporting
Rotary Polioplus & Polio
Eradication!
Take Care
☺ Ramesh Ferris*

Maps: Kayla Beddall
Editor: Joy Wickett
Cover design: Patricia Halladay
Cover photos by Chris Madden.

Back photo: Ramesh Ferris receives a Toronto Blue Jays game jersey from team manager Cito Gaston before the team plays a regular season game at Roger's Place in Toronto, Ontario.

Some of the proceeds from this book will be donated to Rotary International's Polio Plus program and the Ramesh Ferris Foundation for the education, rehabilitation and eradication of Polio.

Photos provided by Ramesh Ferris and Cycle to Walk. Photo of Stephen Harper meeting Ramesh Ferris reproduced with the permission of the Minister of Public Works and Government Services, 2009, and Courtesy of the Privy Council Office.

Order this book online at www.trafford.com or email orders@trafford.com
Most Trafford titles are also available at major online book retailers.

Printed in Victoria, BC, Canada.

ISBN: 978-1-4251-9103-0 (sc)

Our mission is to efficiently provide the world's finest, most comprehensive book publishing service, enabling every author to experience success. To find out how to publish your book, your way, and have it available worldwide, visit us online at www.trafford.com

Trafford rev. 02/18/2010

 www.trafford.com

North America & international
toll-free: 1 888 232 4444 (USA & Canada)
phone: 250 383 6864 ◆ fax: 812 355 4082

My journey and this book are dedicated to
my biological mother, Lakshmi, who resides in India.
My parents, Ron and Jan Ferris,
My brother Matt,
sisters Elisa, Jenny, Rani and Jill,
Brothers-in-law Aaron and Mike,
sister-in-law Lynda.
My community in Whitehorse, Yukon.
And the country I'm so proud to call my home – Canada.

"I contracted polio 25 years after the world had better than a cure – it had a prevention."

Ramesh Ferris

Contents

Introduction xi
1 Roots of the Past 1
2 The Path to Our Destination....................................11
3 The Paralyzer...23
4 Where There's a Will 33
5 The Great Race..43
6 You must be the Change...55
7 One Hand Crank at a Time.......................................61
8 D...as in dumbbell..73
9 We Need to be Really Bothered...............................97
10 Dream Big.. 105
11 Do You Take Donations? 117
12 Every Great Dream... 133
13 The Ever Ascending Path.. 145
14 Victims of our Own Success 151
15 Return to India... 159
Acknowledgements 169
Bibliography 171

Every journey seems so daunting when considering distance and destination but hand cycling across Canada seemed simple and easy when the real goal was to free the world of Polio.

Introduction

✦

Polio holds a special place in our fear.

In December 2008, the Canadian government started running a television ad that opened with the words "This bag could cause a disease outbreak…." It shows a suitcase coming off an airport conveyer and landing on the carousel.

It's a warning to Canadians to be aware of where their luggage has been and what it may contain. It also acknowledges that major threats to the health of Canadians are simply a single plane ride away.

The ad started its run on television just a month after Ramesh Ferris, a 28-year old Polio survivor, completed Cycle to Walk, a 7,140 kilometer cross-country hand cycle from Whitehorse, Yukon to Cape Spear, Newfoundland.

For six months, as he cycled the highways and back roads of Canada, talking to students at schools and re-educating adults at Rotary luncheons, community gathering and church services, Ferris expounded upon one theme – raising awareness of polio and working towards its eradication.

The warning he repeated across the country, "A country is not Polio-free until the world is Polio-free. And as long as there's a single case of Polio, the world is not Polio-free. In a world where travel to any part of the earth is possible, all non-immunized persons are at risk of getting this incurable, highly contagious disease. Polio is one plane flight away."

No sooner had he spoken than the world was hit with the "Swine Flu" pandemic in March 2009. Originating in one country, Mexico, the H1N1 virus spread to 74 countries, affecting almost 30,000 people in just over two months. Primary cause of the rapid spread was identified as airline travel.

A system designed to understand how infectious diseases spread based on air travel patterns was able to accurately predict the spread of the H1N1 virus, but was unable to prevent it. It provides an accurate picture of where diseases will travel, how often and when. However, it can't forecast which disease will be travelling nor where the starting point will be.

Considered endemic in only four countries (Nigeria, Afghanistan, India and Pakistan), in 2008 Polio spread to nine other countries. Incidents around the world tripled. The virus, thought to be non-existent in first world countries, has returned to both the United States and Australia in the past five years.

The United States Center for Disease Control and Prevention (CDC) in 2005 reported two separate incidents of Polio inside the U.S. – both of them believed to be the result of airline passengers arriving on international flights. One was a single unvaccinated American adult male who had apparently been in contact with an infected infant in Costa Rica.

The other was five unvaccinated Amish youngsters in central Minnesota, which created a mild panic. Media publicity raised the specter of children in leg braces and iron lungs, prompting concerned parents to call and email medical authorities for over a month following disclosure. Prior to 2005 there had been no Polio reported in the United States since 1979. The last recorded wild Polio case in the Western Hemisphere was in Peru in 1991. The Americas were declared Polio-free by the World Health Organization (WHO) in 1994.

The Australian incident, in 2007, was a Pakistani student living in Melbourne who returned from a visit to Pakistan. It had been 30 years since Australia's last reported case of Poliomyelitis. The odd thing was that the student had been vaccinated as a child.

The conclusion in the CDC report on the Australian incident stated "Until Polio is completely eradicated, Polio-free regions remain at risk for importation and subsequent transmission." Their recommendation was "Risk for local outbreaks can be minimized by widespread vaccination."

Singapore, a Polio-free area since 2000, reported one case in 2006. The virus was isolated in the sewers of Geneva, Switzerland, in August, 2007 (Europe was declared Polio-free in 2000). The GPEI (Global Polio Eradication Initiative) News reported that "due to high vaccination coverage and good sanitation, detection of the virus is not considered to represent a significant risk of outbreak."

In November, 2008, just two months after Ramesh shared his mission with Prime Minister Stephen Harper and Official Opposition leader Stephane Dion in Ottawa, Ontario, the Canadian government confirmed it would be increasing its contribution to the Global Polio Eradication Initiative from $60 million to $90 million (there were indications prior to Ramesh's visit to Ottawa that the increase might happen, but no definite commitment. Cycle to Walk would be delighted to take credit, but it doesn't. However, the timing of the announcement suggests it may have served as a reminder to the politicians to make the increase).

The Bill and Melinda Gates Foundation and Rotary International, along with the British and German governments, injected a further $630 million in 2009. So far the initiative, started in 1988, has consumed almost four billion dollars along with untold thousands of hours of volunteer and professional efforts without achieving its ultimate goal - making it the most expensive, most intensive, longest enduring health initiative in history.

It is driven by fear. The dread that "the Great Crippler" could re-emerge as a global epidemic and repeat the debilitating effect it had each time it swept through the United States and Canada in the first half of the twentieth century. Polio survivors are the largest disabled group in the world.

In Dryden, Ontario, Ramesh met Roland Swan. Swan grew up in Holland during the Second World War. He had been shot at, bombs exploded next to him and he dealt with war time horrors that young children should never be exposed to.

What terrified him the most in life, after he moved to Canada in the 1950s, was seeing what Polio did to people around him. He couldn't sleep at night knowing that, without warning, he might never walk again, die from asphyxiation or - worst of all - spend the rest of his life in the monstrous iron lung that became the international symbol of the disease.

Reverend David Pritchard of Whitehorse, Yukon, experienced personal suffering and loss because of AIDs, Cholera and Tuberculosis during his time as a husband, parent and missionary in Africa in the 1990s. But it is his memory of the day in 1947 he woke up from an afternoon nap and found he couldn't get out of bed that has never faded.

"After three weeks I was allowed to go home (from the hospital). I had to name all my friends that had been contact with me for a week prior to that day. They were all put in quarantine. I remember begging my mother to allow me to go and meet my friends at the school. One day she said, 'Okay' and I went down to the school. Three boys walked through the gate after classes and one of them looked at me. 'David, is that you?' he asked, 'We thought you were dead.'

Some of the kids I was in the hospital with died. Others ended up with various degrees of withered limbs. And there were some who ended up in the iron lung. I was one of the lucky ones."

Polio preys on the young.

At its worst in the 1950s it closed schools, emptied playgrounds and swimming pools. Children under 16 were banned from entering churches, theatre and any place that people might gather together. Insurance companies sold Polio insurance.

It is Ramesh's vision that Polio – a disease that paralyzed him almost a quarter century after a vaccine had been developed – should be eradicated in his lifetime. He has made it his lifelong mission to pursue that end. His six-month hand cycle trip across Canada was, for him, just a beginning.

The job is 99% complete, but can it ever truly be finished? Is true eradication of any virus even viable?

If it is, it will be only the second time that medicine has freed the world from a viral disease. The first was Smallpox, in 1979.

But has Smallpox truly been eradicated or do we simply not get it anymore? We no longer immunize our children against Smallpox – will they or our grandchildren pay a price because there's a dormant virus out there waiting to thrive again? By letting down our guard, do we provide opportunity for disaster to occur?

There are questions about whether or not the volunteer army of health workers can be maintained long enough to finish the job of eradicating Polio.

"Eradicating a disease is hard, slow, painstaking work," said philanthropist billionaire Bill Gates addressing a Rotary conference in San Diego in January, 2009, "We can't circle a year on the calendar and say we'll end Polio by this date or that date. That sets us up for failure." Failure, he added, would lead to a lessening of the global effort and "a return to the days of tens of thousands of cases per year. That is no alternative at all. We can't let children die because it is fatiguing to save them."

Ramesh, sitting on a high school stage six months earlier with his brace and crutch lying next to him, delivered much the same message.

"Over the next 40 years, the World Health Organization predicts that ten million children will be paralyzed by the effects of Polio unless we complete our mission. Unless we vaccinate every child in every country in the world. We have to finish this job of Polio eradication once and for all. There is no cure for a child with Polio. We cannot let our guard down. We cannot let it be yesterday once more."

Headlines from the Toronto Star, Edmonton Journal, Yukon News and Whitehorse Star announce my successful adoption into the Ferris family in 1982. The photos document progress from casts on my legs to a walker to using crutches.

Roots of the Past

✦

I don't know if there are many people who can say their destiny, their purpose in life, was determined by a specific event that happened to them when they were only six months old.

But I can because it didn't have to happen. It shouldn't have happened at all.

We have the answers. I am reminded every morning, when I wake up and have to put on my brace before I climb out of bed, of the price that ten to twenty million people around the world have to pay because they didn't receive two simple drops of the vaccine at the right time or a needle.

I was an only child. Born in the city of Coimbatore, India, on December 9, 1979. My mother's name is Lakshmi. I never knew my father's first name but his last name was Shanmugan.

My father left while my mother, 18 at the time, was still pregnant with me. He was apparently quite abusive to her.

In India, when the husband leaves the woman – no matter what the situation – it is the woman who is looked at as if there's something wrong with her and she's pretty much shunned from society. When I first communicated with her in 2002, my mother told me she "also was not interested to get married." But I don't think another man could have walked into her life because she had already been rejected by one.

I learned this while I was in India to meet her. We went out to lunch one day and she turned to me.

"This is the first time in my life I have ever been in a restaurant."

Since my biological father left her, she had not really been permitted to be seen in public – especially in the company of a man. She simply couldn't afford to go to a restaurant even if she wanted to. But being with me... her son...that was okay.

My mother never wanted to give me up for adoption but she knew there was something wrong because, after a year, I still couldn't walk and was very sick. When she realized her income and social standing wouldn't permit her to give me the type of care I needed, she moved in with my grandparents.

It's a single room in a hut-like building. There are eight rooms in the house – each occupied by a different family. In our room there was one bed for my grandparents and one for my mother and myself. They shared a kitchen area with the occupants of the other rooms and a common bathroom.

My grandmother and mother still live in that same room in that same building. They sleep together on a single mattress. My grandfather died about 15 years ago.

I don't know what my mother did for a living back then. Today she works at a metal furniture shop, assembling furniture. She earns about 30 rupees (about $1.00 U.S.) per day. My grandmother is making dosa (an Indian bread) to sell in the market.

Eventually having me living there in that room just got to be too much for them.

After a year and a half she made one of the biggest decisions of her life – to take me to the orphanage. Technically I wasn't an orphan, but she had to give me up so that I could get help. So I might be able to walk. And her life would stay the same.

In the first letter I ever received from her she wrote "I wanted to tell you due to my family situation I gave you in adoption. Other than that I have no other reason. From day one (when you went in adoption) till today, I am thinking of you. Where ever you are, you should be happy, that is our wish."

She decided to give me to an orphanage, Families for Children, in Podanur - a small village a couple of miles outside Coimbatore.

When I was stepping out of my biological mother's home in 2002, I was startled when one of my uncles started to cry. He was a sort-of tough-looking guy and the tears looked out of place. So I asked the translator – everyone there spoke Tamil, but no English, so I needed a translator with me – I asked him to ask my uncle what was the matter.

The translator said to me that my mother, my aunt and he (my crying uncle) were the ones who dropped me off at the orphanage. He was just overwhelmed to see me 20 years later.

Sandra Simpson, who lives in Montreal, is the founder of Families for Children. She set up two orphanages – one in Bangladesh and one in India - and still supervises them today despite having had a bout with cancer recently. She received the Order of Canada a few years ago for the impact that her work with Families for Children has had in this area of the world.

In Canada, when I think of an orphanage, I think of the stereotypical Oliver Twist. Dirty kids. Tattered clothes. Gruel. "Please sir, could I have some more?" But that wasn't the case at all for the orphanage that I was given to.

It had, and still has, about 600 kids and staff living in six large houses spread out over a couple of blocks. The kids sleep on mats on the floor although there are beds in the special care facility. It's very basic. They eat together. They milk their goats at six in the morning. There are a few brightly colored balls and various other toys. A lot of emphasis is put on education and chores. And respect for people.

All children are accepted into the orphanage regardless of physical or cognitive challenges and all of them come from destitute families.

While I was visiting in 2002, the kids were mostly happy and looked well cared for. But the braces and medical equipment for the Polio kids and children with disabilities weren't anywhere near what I was used to seeing in Canada. They're doing well with what they have but I know how much better it can be.

When my mother took me to the orphanage I still wasn't walking. I wasn't officially diagnosed while I was there – just under two years – and even during the adoption process it was unclear what I was suffering from. They said it "could" be Polio, but there was no firm diagnosis until after my arrival in Canada.

A lot of people thought I might be mentally retarded because my development was so slow. It was actually a notation in my medical file. One day a man by the name of John Sayer, took me to a doctors' appointment.

John and his wife were volunteers at the orphanage. They volunteered several times over the years after he had retired from teaching in Canada. One of his jobs was to take the kids to their medical appointments.

I was sitting on his knee in the waiting room and I reached up and pulled a pen from his pocket. Then I took it apart, looked at it, put it back together and put it back in his pocket. I was two years old.

At that point John realized that the only intellectual limitation I had was a lack of stimulation. Because of my legs I was unable to learn to walk or move about and my experience had been extremely limited.

Nobody could possibly have known at that time exactly how important those few minutes in the waiting room were going to be for me. John told Sandra Simpson about the pen and it played a significant role in the decision she made concerning my future.

In October, 1981, she contacted a family in Canada, Ron and Jan Ferris, who had already adopted two girls, Jenny and Rani, from Families for Children and were looking for one more child. Sandra is the one who identified all of us kids to go to the Ferris family.

Me, she selected because of my "could be" polio. My parents she picked because she anticipated there would be challenges getting a seriously handicapped child into Canada and she needed a high profile family who might be able to pull it off.

My Dad (Ron Ferris) had just been elected as the Bishop of the Anglican Diocese of Yukon in 1981. He and my Mom (Jan Ferris) had also adopted a total of five children starting in 1970. Jenny and Rani from Families for Children and three, Elisa, Matthew and Jill, through the Children's Aid Society in Ontario. They have no biological children of their own.

Interestingly enough, the "could be" Polio didn't really seem to be the major issue. It was the reason used by the immigration department, but it was the notation of "mentally retarded" in my medical file that appears to have been the real problem. It was that which prompted the Canadian government to exercise Section 19 of the Immigration Act prohibiting me from entering the country because I may cause excessive demand on health and social services.

To this day I feel very strongly that this section of the act is prejudicial and should not be exercised on children who are 18 years old or younger.

I was examined in India in June, 1982, for my Canadian visa, but it wasn't until September 14 that the immigration department informed the Ferris family that their application was denied – just two weeks before I was supposed to make the trip to Canada.

When my parents found out my entry had been denied, they turned to a couple of Whitehorse journalists, Sumari Sugomoto and Colin Hoath of the Canadian Broadcasting Corporation. They were very influential in getting national attention focused on my adoption case - on both radio and in newspapers across the country.

After the immigration department defended their position, my father responded, "I don't think a handful of children adopted from abroad will be a threat to the health care system. Here is a child who has a very good reason to be in Canada, who has a family who will love him."

The adverse publicity apparently made political life a little uncomfortable for Federal Immigration Minister Lloyd Axworthy. When the appeal from my father arrived on his desk, he picked up his phone and called Sandra Simpson in Montreal.

"What's the situation with this Ramesh boy?" he asked her.

She said, "Just a second" and handed the phone to John Sayer who happened to be sitting at her kitchen table having a cup of coffee. He told Axworthy the story of the pen and shortly after that a special ministerial permit was issued allowing me to enter the country.

I'm fortunate John chose that story to tell and not the one about the time he had to reprimand me for throwing stones at another boy in the orphanage.

I arrived at Edmonton International Airport - my father calls it "the delivery room" – on September 27, 1982, and became the first international adoption in the Yukon Territory.

While my Dad was waiting for me to come off the plane the Toronto Maple Leafs hockey team exited first. The media, he told me, totally ignored them. Imagine ignoring a professional hockey team in Canada! When the flight attendant come out of the plane with me in her arms, that's when the media frenzy began.

I don't remember hearing them, I was pretty young at the time, but I do know the first words my Dad ever spoke to me, "How are you doing eh?" Then he kissed me on the forehead.

Neither of my parents had even seen me before that day. My parents were connected to Sandra Simpson and they had already adopted two children from her orphanage. But they had never gone to India.

They never saw any of us before adoption. They had just read about us from what Sandra had given them.

My Mom wasn't in Edmonton to pick me up. She had five other kids to look after in Whitehorse but I remember having an incredibly strong bond with her. We had that relationship because of our time together as the result of my medical issues. It was shortly after arriving that it was confirmed that I do indeed have Polio and had probably contracted it at about six months of age.

It affected more than my legs. I had pneumonia nine times before I was eleven. My lungs were always congested with fluid and my mother always had to do percussion (drumming with hands on the chest and back to provoke draining in the lungs).

I was tested for hearing loss. Had speech therapy because I had all these problems with my S's and TH's. I did some work with the child development center in Whitehorse. They had me repeat "She sells sea shells by the sea shore" over and over and over again.

The polio made me slower in almost all areas of development.

I learned to walk at three and a half – after surgery at Vancouver General Hospital. When it was time to take my casts off the doctors were amazed because I had worn holes right through them where my legs dragged behind me. Even when I was young I wasn't going to let something as simple as not being able to walk slow me down.

When I first learned to walk I had two braces, one on each leg, and a walker. There was a fire hydrant about a block down Firth Road, where we lived, and it would take me 45 minutes to walk one way.

That same route was where we started Cycle to Walk on April 10, 2008. In my hand I carried the first brace I ever used – the brace that enabled me to walk to the fire hydrant as a child. The walk in 2008, from the home where I grew up to the fire hydrant where my hand cycle was parked, took only two minutes.

My first paying job was a paper route for the Whitehorse Star. I had 31 papers. There were too many for me to do all at once. So I'd put half down. Do half the route. Come back. Pick up the rest and do the other half. But I resolved to do it and to do it well. I made lots of tips from people who saw my determination, the braces and the crutches and wanted to reward that.

I shoveled snow from neighbors' driveways along Firth Road. Right from the beginning I focused on what I could do, not what I couldn't do.

There's nothing I regret about my family life. I have a very loving, supportive family. All of us kids were encouraged to do our thing...to be our own person. To achieve what we could achieve. To set our own dreams. And we always laughed. We are all just really proud that we are part of the Ferris family.

I've only ever known my father as a Bishop. Growing up in a Anglican home, church definitely played a role in our lives. He travelled a lot. He loved and supported me as much as my mother, but he had to be away frequently because of his work.

He would call me when he was in Toronto and say "Hello son. I can't hear you very well as I'm behind home plate at the Toronto Blue Jays game." I thought of those calls when I cycled onto the field before a Blue Jays game at the Rogers Center in Toronto in 2008. It's too bad I didn't think to call him while I was there and say "Hello Dad. I can't hear you..."

However I have to say, it wasn't the wonderful adoption story as far as... yes, I was standing and walking and I had a wonderful family...but then you get what society paints as a societal normal person – and it's not a person who's been adopted, walks with a limp and uses crutches.

There were some really nasty times for me growing up in the Yukon.

Being non-First Nations, but being colored. My parents were both vanilla and I was chocolate. Lots of school kids would see us together and ask me 'Why the color difference?" The Yukon wasn't used to blended families yet!

Being a person who is catagorized as "disabled" and having a father who is a bishop.

In elementary school, gym class was horrible. There wasn't one teacher who said 'Let's look at what Jonathan (I was given a Christian name, Jonathan David Ramesh Ferris, when I was adopted and Jonathan was how I was known until after my visit to India in 2002) can do and try to be all at the same level.' For instance, wheelchair basketball or handcycling – none of that was ever thought of.

It was "OK Jonathan. You can go home for the rest of the day or go to the library to read a book, or do what you want to do - It's free time for you because you can't run like everyone else." In high school, I just didn't pick gym as a class. I picked things I could do.

In school there were nightmare situations where kids would call me "cripple." They would steal my crutches. They would kick my crutches out from under me.

There were times when I wouldn't be picked for things. My friends would run away from me. Quite often I would find myself walking alone because no one wanted to walk the same pace as the black, crippled guy. Which is ironic, because I'm not black. I'm chocolate. I'm Indian.

There were a lot of hurtful times. But I always smiled so no one ever knew how much it hurt.

There were some really harsh things done. A boy pushed me down and rode over my legs with his bicycle.

Once somebody knocked me down, took my crutches and put them in the garbage. I just had to lie there until someone got up the courage to say 'that's not right', take my crutches out of the garbage and give them to me.

It felt like ages before someone actually did get the crutches but it probably wasn't that long. And a couple of people walked by before they were returned.

I did react sometimes. I hit people with my crutches as a response. There was one incident where someone tried to push me down a hill and I ended up biting his leg. We went to the principal's office and I remember the principal asking me,

"Are you a dog?"

"No," I replied

"Well, only dogs bite."

I wasn't strong enough to explain 'Well, so-and-so called me this' or 'made me feel like this.' I was so ashamed of being a person with a disability I didn't really ever want to use that as an excuse for my actions. I had to pick up garbage around the school for a week after that.

There was a time when I was angry and resentful that this disability had to happen to me. I wasn't always the most academically inclined student – just ask my parents! There were so many social issues I had to address. The biggest challenge for me was to ensure I fit in just so I wasn't going to be made fun of.

In high school I watched my friends go out on dates and I just sort of "hung out" on my own or as a third person on the date. I heard so many times from my mother and other people, "Oh. You're such a great guy. I don't know why anyone's not going out with you."

The truth is we lived in a very judging world. It's sad that we still live in a discriminating world where people look more at outside appearances than what they have to share inside.

7

I found there were some people who could see me for who I was and took the time to listen to what I had to say and recognize any gifts I had to share. There are a few who I still have friendships with from those days. Stephen Reid – he now teaches in Whitehorse. And Sara Pyke. She was the first girl who ever really looked at me and took the time to listen to me.

When I was in grade eight we moved to Berkeley, California, for six months where my father was working on his doctorate in ministry. In California, people didn't look at my limited mobility. They saw just me. They called me "Captain Canada." I was okay with that. I was proud to be from Canada.

It was a wonderful experience to be immersed in the cultural melting pot. People in California thought I was Hispanic. It was amazing to go from being Black to being Hispanic. And none of it is correct. I'm Indian.

That experience helped me to focus on my abilities rather than my disabilities. When we returned to Whitehorse I got into the leadership programs at Porter Creek Junior High because of an inspirational guidance counselor, Flo Kitz, who has since passed away from cancer. I was elected president of the student council.

I didn't graduate from high school in the Yukon. My father was transferred to Sault Ste. Marie, Ontario, when I was 15 years old so I graduated from Sir James Dunn High School in "the Soo."

When we moved to Sault Ste. Marie I had a goatee and long hair and people thought I was older than I actually was.

For some reason I got a lot of respect right away. They thought I was black there too. Many of them also thought I wasn't a student, but a "narc" or undercover cop of some sort. I have no idea why they would think that.

They were all amazed by the size of my upper body. The size came from my crutches and body shape. There was a time my brother was into lifting weights, so I got into it. But I never really liked it. I'd do a couple of lifts and think 'Okay. That's good...BORING!'

I was being judged, but not for braces and crutches. I got the feeling there was more respect for me from my peers – but there was still a lot of the same issues. I was always trying to catch up to the crowd.

Again I picked things I knew I could do. I exercised my leadership skills by getting involved with the church community and became president of the Anglican Diocese of Algoma Deanery Youth Unit. We were responsible for Bible studies, fund raising, retreats. I was inspired by seeing other young people in the church. But I was also ashamed.

At that age I wasn't about to tell anyone I was going to church on Sunday mornings and my father was a bishop. I would be out partying on Friday night, but Saturday morning I'd be leading a meeting for the Youth Unit in the basement of a church.

I formed a lot of good friendships through the church. I met my first serious girl friend – Elizabeth Soloway. We had a long distance relationship. She lived in Thunder Bay and I lived in the Soo. She was actually the first woman I went out with and we had a close relationship. I know we annoyed my father with the long distance phone calls because he had to pay for them.

When we broke up, it was a bad break up. I went out with her at a time in my life when I was still concerned with my body image and put a lot of blame on her that I am the way I am. I've grown up a lot since then and realize I put a lot of things on her I shouldn't have.

Cycle to Walk has been a lot of healing and a lot of connecting with the past. I met her when I was in Thunder Bay and we talked about that. It was a wonderful opportunity and she's proud of how far I've come.

Even as late as 2004, I would never wear shorts because I was too ashamed of what people would think. It really wasn't until after the trip to India that I began to realize 'Gosh. I'm alive. And I'm walking. And this was all given to me by a woman (my biological mother) who gave me up so I could have a better life.'

I do wear shorts now but even today – the body shape thing. When I ask women out and they say "no" – it's still in the back of my head. If a relationship doesn't work out, I always wonder…

It still makes me angry occasionally. I think I was angry for many years but I became so appreciative of what I had after I went back to India in 2002.

That was a big turning point in my life.

I've always been a person who – if I envision a goal – for some reason it always happens. I just know that everything I've ever wanted has worked out and I don't mean that in an arrogant or cocky way. I say that in the sense that I believe that God has always provided for me and that I'm on the right journey – His journey. If there's an obstacle that has been put in my way, it's there for me to move around or grow past so I can experience other people and other things.

I was unable to walk like other people – but I was determined to walk. I was in swimming lessons. I couldn't swim as well or as fast as everyone else, but I finished. I wasn't able to use my legs or feet to drive a car so I got hand controls.

Something as simple as opening a door. How much of the effort of pulling the door open is in your leg muscles? More than you realize.

One comment people say to me is 'I wouldn't want to arm wrestle with you.' The reality is that anybody could beat me at arm wrestling because they don't realize how much leg strength and balance is required in an arm wrestle. But that's one misconception I won't correct.

Family and friends outside my biological mother's home in Coimbatore, India. My mother, Lakshmi, is to my right and my grandmother Chellanewal, with her white hair is to my left. There were so many I can't remember who the others are.

The Path to Our Destination

✦

When I finished my final year at Confederation College in Thunder Bay – in 2001 with a diploma in social work – I took some time off and went to visit my parents in Sault Ste. Marie. Before I returned to Thunder Bay to pack up my room, my Dad presented me with an official notarized paper from India. It was the document that assigned me from my biological mother to the orphanage.

The entire drive back to Thunder Bay I kept thinking about it. Somewhere on that journey I thought I might like to meet her some day… No…I knew I had to meet her.

I was about to return to the Yukon. I had two jobs in Whitehorse. One was with the Yukon Government doing residential counseling with kids in receiving homes and the other was as a support worker for adults with intellectual disabilities in an agency called Tegatha Oh Zheh

It was a hectic time, moving across the country, starting new jobs, dealing with the realities of every day life like paying down student debt and covering the rent, trying to reconnect with old friends and make new ones.

Feeding myself was, and still is, a problem because I don't cook. Growing up we always knew dinner was ready when the smoke detector in the kitchen was going off and Mom was frantically waving a tea towel to clear the smoke out of the air. I like to say that I've adopted her motto for cooking – the best recipe is a menu.

Somewhere in that confusion I found time to send an e-mail to Sandra Simpson in Montreal, the founder of the orphanage in

Coimbatore, expressing my interest in connecting with my biological mother.

Sandra responded immediately. She said "That's great. Just be prepared to be asked for citizenship and money."

I didn't care. I just wanted to meet my biological mother. Sandra could have told me anything, but it wouldn't have mattered. This is what I wanted to do. I decided to write to my mother through the orphanage.

What do you say to a biological mother you've never met?

I focused on introducing myself and describing what my life had become because of her courage. Thanking her and expressing my interest in meeting her one day. For her to see me walking. It was pretty short. Just one or two pages.

Just before Christmas, 2001, I received a response from her.

It had been sent by Families for Children to my parent's address in Sault Ste. Marie because I had still been moving when I wrote my letter and didn't have an address of my own at the time. The letter is written in Tamil. It was accompanied by an English translation from a woman, Kalyani, who works at the orphanage.

"Dear Son Ramesh (Jonathan)

I am Lakshmi your mother writing to you. Here we are doing fine. How is your Father? Mother? Yourself? Your brother and sister? Myself and your Grandmother are very eager to know about it. We received your letter and I was very happy to receive it…I would like to say that you were the only son for me. No brother or sister for you.

I am living with my mother…Myself and my mother are very eager to see you in person but it is not possible for us to come and visit you as you in abroad and it is very far from here. If possible you can try and come to India to see us. If you are not able to visit us you can get in touch with us through phone or mail us. We have a phone in our work place. You have to tell my name while you call and have to speak to me between 9 a.m. and 6 p.m. (Indian time).

My father passed away 15 years ago and now my mother is also sick. So I was not able to reply to your letter immediately. Myself and your granny are much eager to see you.

If you have any idea to visit us, please discuss it with your Mother and Father before taking any decision. Please convey my regards to your parents. I have enclosed photos of our family as well as my photo and grandmother's too. I would like to see your family photo and yours separately in the next letter.

Please reply as soon as you receive my letter. We are very eagerly waiting for your reply.

Your mother Lakshmi and Grandmother Chellanewal "

When I read this letter, there was no longer any doubt at all in my mind. I knew I was going to meet her.

I called my parents and told them. They were very supportive and very practical. They grew up in a time of poverty so they're always concerned about debt. They've always been that way.

"Okay. We love you and we support you in your decision," my Dad said, "But you have loans from school and we think you should take care of that first."

However I knew this was my decision and that debt is always going to be there. I'm always going to be in the hole for some reason. Buying a car. Taking out a mortgage. Whatever. I just had to keep my priorities in focus. I chose to be in debt longer so I could meet my mother.

I was making good money so, even with the loan payments and living costs, it was easy to earn the money for a plane ticket to India within a month.

I asked my sister Rani to come with me. She had been unable to find her birth parents through the orphanage. I asked her "How do you feel about that?"

"I'm fine," she told me, "I'm here to support you. I'm excited for you."

I approached Jenny, but she didn't want to go. This just wasn't where she was in her life.

In the end, Rani and Matt decided to go with me. It was a journey for all of us. I had envisioned that I was going to be the only one there when I met my birth mother. I never envisioned my brother and sister to be there with me.

I wrote my birth mother and told her I was coming to India. But I didn't give her a specific date. I didn't want her to be thinking about it every day and I wasn't sure exactly how I wanted it to happen.

I don't remember much about the flight to get there. Just that it took a long time. Thirty hours, from Whitehorse to Los Angeles, to Taipei, Singapore and Chennai (formerly known as Madras) in India, where we had a short overnight chance to sleep before flying one hour south to Coimbatore.

The first thing we did was drive out to the orphanage in Podanur. We didn't talk a lot. We were so intent on seeing the orphanage that we really didn't notice the culture around us. We were aware of it, we just didn't see it. I just kept thinking 'Wow. This is the city where I was born. And this is where I lived.'

When we got to the orphanage I was surprised because everyone, the staff, the children, were so respectful. They were so happy that Rani and Matt would take the time to travel to the orphanage to visit with them. They called us "brother" and "sister" and they were just so cheerfull. Smiling all the time. They were excited to share with us their talents of music and dance. They were happy to carry the luggage and or offer us food. They were just so ready to share themselves with us.

INDIA

June 2002
November 2008

I guess what I really saw in those first days was the power of the human spirit. There were very few materialistic items and they didn't need anything more. They had themselves. They had shelter. Food. Clothing. And they had people around them who loved them. I could see that in their interaction.

It was wonderful to be in a world where children didn't care about television, video games, CDs, or the latest fashions. Having a tidy uniform and going to school every day was exciting for them.

Matt had brought a small rubber ball – the type of ball you can find in any North American toy store or five-and-dime. They played with that ball for hours. This was a rubber ball! It wasn't an expensive Lego set. It was a rubber ball.

I also met the young boy I had been sponsoring at the orphanage. He was ten years old at the time. Every year I still donate $150 towards the cost of providing him with food, clothing and an education.

One woman about my age started to cry when she saw me. She lived in the orphanage at the same time I did and we played together. She had never been adopted. The kids who weren't adopted out grew up in the orphanage then stayed on as adult staff members.

There were staff members who had been in their teens or were young adults when I was there, who still remembered me.

One, her name is Jay Mary – a wonderful lady – said "I remember you Ramesh. You were a playful child. Always smiling." That was special for me to hear. Finding out what I was like at the orphanage because that was something my parents would not have known.

While we were there we decided to go to the hospital where Rani was born. There was Rani, Matt, myself, some translators and a couple of orphanage staff talking about Rani's adoption. A nurse overhearing our conversation, turned to us, said "Just a minute" and headed off into the hospital.

A frail woman came down the hall wearing a white doctor's jacket. She was in her late eighties and wasn't quite sure why the nurse was introducing her to us. Until Rani was introduced, then a tear came to her eye.

"One week ago," she told us, "I was thinking about this child I delivered because her mother abandoned her into my care. I named her Rani and I put her into the orphanage. And one week later you walk in here and you're Rani."

Rani was stunned and she started to cry.

"You are the doctor that delivered me?!"

"Yes. I am."

For Rani, this was the most wonderful part of this trip. We were there to meet my birth mother and she was able to find something from her past as well. And maybe something she was looking for.

I was still trying to figure out just how I wanted my meeting to go. We had already been in Coimbatore for a few days and still hadn't made any move to go beyond the orphanage.

I set up the first meeting for myself to travel to her home rather than meeting at the orphanage. That way I would have control and could decide when enough was enough. If things weren't comfortable or didn't work out, then I could dictate when I would leave.

Rani and Matt stayed at the orphanage. It was important for me to have that moment for myself when we met. I was anxious. Nervous. Excited. Scared. Most of all I was just prepared to thank a woman for a decision she made almost 30 years ago.

It was about a 30 minute drive from the orphanage to her home. All the way I just kept repeating to myself "I'm going to meet my mother. I'm going to meet my biological mother." It was very surreal. We drove through small villages with hundreds of people around, tons of goats and streets crowded with noisy, smelly Corsa buses.

We drove past this lady with a shopping bag. I was so wound up with anticipation I just didn't see her. The driver, Money, who was from the orphanage, turned to me and said, "I think that was your mother we just drove by."

When we got out of the vehicle, there were relatives – aunts and uncles – and neighbours, about thirty in total, gathered around the front of her building and she was actually just walking up the road with this bag. She immediately handed the bag to a family member then started to cry, gave me a huge hug and a kiss.

At first, I gave her a handshake because I really didn't know how to greet her. I said something like "Oh. Good to meet you." I smiled because I was happy to be there but I didn't feel the need to give her a hug. I was meeting a stranger. Now, in hindsight, I wish I could go back and do it over again.

I couldn't take my eyes off her physical features and reflecting them back onto myself. Like, 'Oh my gosh. No wonder I'm short.' Or 'This is where I got my nose from.' Growing up in Canada and being around my friends I always heard "Oh they look like their mom." Or "You can see they're so-and-so's kids." I could never share that.

For the first time in my life I was looking at this woman who looked so much like me, I couldn't stop staring at her.

We went into her room. It was quite small. They were so thrilled to share photos. There was a big picture of my grandfather, who died about 15 years before I went to India. I looked at his photo and at my uncle's pictures and I thought 'Oh my goodness. I'm going to have white hair!' Even my mother has white hair.

What I wasn't prepared for was seeing the emotional and physical attachment that my mother had for me.

She always wanted to hold my hand. To be close to me and that made me uncomfortable because I just didn't have that connection to her. I felt quite smothered in affection.

She was overjoyed. Me. Her son. A Canadian citizen. I was walking and that made her really proud. And for me to see where she lived. By Canadian standards it was a very impoverished place.

Her whole existence was based on survival. Their lives went on and on and nothing much changes. We expect change here (in Canada) and they had no such expectations. It had been easy for the orphanage to find her because she was so poor she would never be able to move. Even in Canada the poor can move! In India you're born poor and you stay poor, or you're one of the few who will get out of the system, or you're born wealthy.

For the first time in her life she was probably able to focus on what she had done for someone else rather than the day-to-day grind of survival.

Here I was, able to walk to her doorstep and give her a handshake. I should have given her a hug. Here, in real life, was the one person who had ensured I would have the opportunity for a better life.

There were aunts, uncles, neighbours, cousins, a couple of translators and the driver at that first meeting. We were there about an hour. Over 11 days we had a total of five visits.

She took me on a tour of where she worked and I could see her pride. You could see it in her eyes and hear it in her voice when she introduced me.

"This is my son."

One of the things that this kind of event does is open up the question, "So what happens now." What role do I want my biological mother to play in my life and what role do I play in hers?

That's where I'm completely torn. I don't know the answers. Even now, a number of years after meeting her, I still don't know. What I've done is put it on my personal backburner.

Sandra Simpson was right about that. I think my aunts wanted something from me. I know my grandmother wanted something. "Okay. Now that you've found us, what are you going to do for us?"

I was really stuck then and still am today. I can't afford to support both myself and my biological family. I don't have the finances to fly to India every year or put a thousand dollars in a bank account every few months. It's those debts that my parents were concerned about when I told them I was going to India.

I do know that later on, when I'm more financially established, I want to continue to grow in my relationship with my biological family through visits there and them coming here. But I have no place for them to come to. I want to show them that I have a home, not welcome them with "This is the room I rent in this house."

When we flew out the entire family came to the airport to say good-bye. It made me feel better that, yeah, I'd done the right thing in contacting my family.

It was after meeting my biological mother and spending some time at the orphanage that I started to see the reality of Polio. I didn't see a lot of Polio survivors. I saw a few, but that was all I needed to see. I have to admit that, at the time, I wasn't looking for them. That's not why I was there. I was there to meet my mother, and get absorbed into the city where I was born.

I actually didn't see any Polio victims at all until I went to the orphanage, but the kids at the orphanage are looked after. They have crutches, but don't wear braces.

When I left the orphanage for a walk I saw people sitting on the ground with skinny legs curled or twisted up underneath them. I saw one or two who were crawling with cut up tire pieces on their knees and wearing sandals like gloves on their hands. When I first saw them I didn't realize they were Polio victims. It actually wasn't until one day near the orphanage, when I was specifically introduced to a Polio victim who wasn't living at the orphanage, that I realized what I had been looking at.

It was also the first time I had ever seen a hand cycle. I was amazed at the capabilities and ingenuity of the man on the hand cycle. He had designed and built it himself. His legs were like mine, but they were twisted underneath him and his back was hunched. The effects of Polio were much more severe for him than me.

I asked him if I could try his cycle and that was my very first time on one. It didn't work so well for me because it had been designed for him so my first thought wasn't 'Cool. I'm on a hand cycle.' It was more along the lines of 'Whoa. How do you make this thing work?'

My decision to do something for Polio didn't happen until after I returned to Canada and started to reflect back on my visit.

People think that I went to India, saw all these "crawlers" and that's where Cycle to Walk came from. But the truth is that it took a couple of years of processing – having actually seen Polio survivors in India then researching it here in Canada.

I had just met my birth mother and thanked her for what she did, but it didn't really register with me how I fit in with Polio survivors. It wasn't until I was able to realize what my life could have been that the first thoughts that eventually became Cycle to Walk actually occurred.

When I returned to Whitehorse I didn't think anyone would be there to greet me. But when I came into the terminal some of my friends were all hiding behind a wall and they jumped out shouting "JONATHAN!" They were all excited about the journey and took me down to the bar at the Capital Hotel to celebrate my return and hear the stories.

For me it was a cultural crash. I had just completed one of the most intense, intimate periods of my personal life and I was here, having a bar discussion about it over a beer just minutes after getting off the plane. For me, that was a problem.

People cared about the journey, but, for them, it seemed like a 20-minute thing then move on with life. Sitting there in the bar – surrounded by my friends and my colleagues from work I started to wonder, 'What am I doing here?' I had been so emotionally impacted by the trip and I looked around at everyone in the bar. I suddenly realized, 'there's a real problem here.'

I turned to the person next to me and said, "I need to go. This isn't good." And I walked out.

I haven't been the same since.

Slowly I detached myself from my friends. I had to take a lot of private time for myself to think about my life and that's when I decided to research Polio. I don't know if my friends understood what was happening to me. I like to believe they did.

I was looking for more support than what they could give. I realized at that point that I was on my own personal journey and I was going to have to be okay to be alone with this. The people who were around me would have to be there if I needed them but ultimately it was going to be my own challenge. I think I became comfortable with that. That was my world and I had to learn how to cope with it.

A part of me was upset about the fact that I don't know my culture. I don't know the language. The customs. The religion. What I did learn was Canadian culture. North American food. The Anglican faith.

I asked 'how come I was never given any of this?', but that was an initial reaction. On reflection, in the Yukon, in the 1980s, adoption really wasn't as sophisticated as it is now. There wasn't the amount of education about keeping contact with birth cultures. There wasn't a large cultural community in Whitehorse back then - in truth, I don't think there was any other people from India in the Yukon at all at that time. There was no way they could introduce me to Indian culture.

I made the decision to stop using my Christian name of Jonathan and went back to my original name, Ramesh.

I started swimming. Quit smoking – is that a bad thing to admit in this day and age? I knew I wanted to do something but just didn't know what or why.

I got very involved in wheelchair sports both in the Yukon and nationally. I started wheelchair basketball in the Yukon. Taught it and coached it. I was involved with the Canadian Wheelchair Basketball Association, the

Active Living Alliance for Canadians with a Disability and the Canadian Wheelchair Sports Association.

In the summer of 2005, I and my dog Zaeda, a Tsitzu Pomeranian cross who came to me via a break-up with a girlfriend, camped at Wolf Creek campground about ten miles south of Whitehorse. Every morning I commuted to the adult services unit where I was working as a case manager for social assistance. After work I would have a shower at my house, then go back to the campground in the evening for dinner and to sleep.

I was sitting on a stump in the late evening, just watching the rolling current of the creek, the eroding sides, the mini-currents created by small back eddies and calm spots along the side of the creek when I remembered the man on the hand cycle in Coimbatore.

"Hand cycling! That's what I'll do."

I also kept thinking about India and knew I wanted to do something about helping Polio survivors. Nobody should be condemned to live in the dirt. They should have access to simple aids like braces and forearm crutches.

I thought about my personal inspirations in life. Terry Fox. Rick Hansen. Driven people. People with a dream. People who didn't let physical obstacles stand in the way of achieving their dream. And just like that, it all came together. I'd hand cycle across Canada.

I didn't have a hand cycle and I hadn't cycled a kilometer in my life. I couldn't even change a tire. I couldn't afford it and would probably have to quit work to do it. But I knew I wanted to hand cycle across Canada.

I started researching hand cycling on the internet. I talked to James Black at Medichair Yukon because they are the Yukon dealership for hand cycles.

Later that summer, during my brother's wedding at Ball's Falls, Ontario, I mentioned the idea to my family. Matt was very supportive.

"Go talk to Rotary," he told me, "They're a big organization and Polio is a big thing for them."

The first thing my Dad said was "Well, knowing you, you'll probably do it. You'll probably find some way to get it done." Then, being the eternal pragmatist, he added, "You know you still owe a lot of money for school. After your bike trip, you should think about getting a job and paying your debt off."

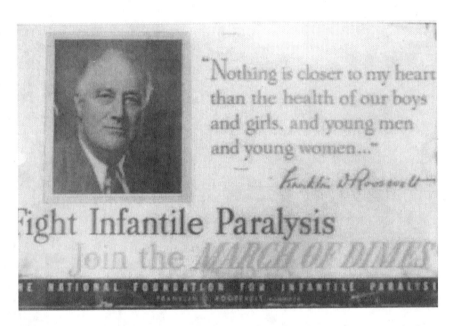

A "March of Dimes" poster uses the words of Franklin Delano Roosevelt to urge people to join in the war against Polio. Roosevelt was the driving force behind the National Foundation for Infantile Paralysis.

The Paralyzer

✦

A brief history of Polio, FDR and the March of Dimes

Had Franklin Delano Roosevelt not been allowed to go home, his political ambitions were such that he might have ended up as the Prime Minister of Canada rather than the President of the United States. His love of Canada and Canada's affection for him prompted Ottawa Mayor Staley Lewis, following a speech by Roosevelt in August, 1943, to say "I hope I will not be misunderstood when I say many Canadians affectionately call you 'our president.'"

Franklin Delano Roosevelt, known to historians as FDR, was 39 years old in the summer of 1921 at the family vacation home on Campobello Island, just off the southern coast of New Brunswick. At the start of the holiday he was a physically powerful man who played lawn tennis and polo, golf, was a rower and a target shooter. His daily morning routine started with a two mile jog, followed by a swim across a fresh water lake and a splash in the Bay of Fundy. Then he would reverse the course to get back home. He was considered a fine specimen of what a fit man should look like and exuded an air of arrogant superiority about his physical appearance.

Early in the morning of August 8, he felt like he was coming down with a minor flu - running a mild fever, suffering from aching muscles and low energy. By the afternoon he was paralyzed from the waist down. It was initially diagnosed as a possible blood clot from an injury and the prognosis was good – any effects should be just temporary. A week later the diagnosis was changed to Poliomyelitis. He never walked again.

When U.S. immigration officials heard the diagnosis, they initially refused to admit him back into the United States. They didn't really understand what he had but the possible threat he posed to the American public was, in their minds, very evident in his physical condition. (Even as recently as 2009, American immigration officers still had no understanding of the virus. When Ramesh Ferris entered the United States on a visit to Warm Springs, Georgia, he was asked "Will you afflict Polio on the citizens of the United States?")

Through his legal and political connections FDR was able to get the decision overturned and return home.

He is lauded as one of the greatest presidents the United States ever had - his New Deal, which was the groundwork for pulling both the U.S. and Canada out of the Great Depression, and his leadership during the Second World War mostly defined his role in history.

However, it was his experience with extreme suffering that truly made him a man of the people. It made him less arrogant and smug, less superficial, more focused and much more interesting. He used it to inspire others, often pushing his wheelchair through hospital wards where severely wounded soldiers awaited surgery and rehabilitation. He wanted to show them what could be accomplished even if they lost some aspect of their mobility.

It was his unswerving faith that Polio could be defeated and he would be cured. That belief turned him into a champion in the war against Polio and gave him his most fitting monument – his portrait on the American dime.

Poliomyelitis (the name was shortened to "Polio" by newspapers trying to fit it into headlines), known as 'The Twentieth Century Plague', has apparently been around for a long time. The oldest known possible historical reference was a stone stele, or tablet, produced during the 18th dynasty in ancient Egypt – over 3,000 years ago. The carving shows a priest using a crutch and walking with the "dropped foot" of Polio victims.

The mummy of the Pharoah Siptah, who reigned over Egypt from 1197 BC to 1191 BC, has a deformed left leg. The foot had been held vertical, in the dropped foot position, by a shortened Achilles Tendon. Some medical historians point to Polio as the cause while others prefer Cerebral Palsy.

Health records for the Emperor of Rome, Claudius, list physical ailments for the last 13 years of his life (41-54 AD) consistent with symptoms of Polio.

Poliomyelitis is a highly contagious intestinal virus that preys upon gaps in an individual's immune system. It is spread by person-to-person contact, primarily via fecal matter (diaper changes, contaminated water, poor personal hygiene etc) although the U.S. Centers for Disease Control and Prevention (CDC) also suggests oral/nasal secretions as possible transmitters.

Pregnant women can transmit the virus to their unborn children, but the fetus doesn't appear to be affected by either maternal infection or vaccination. The mother can also pass antibodies to the fetus providing it with short term immunity during the first few months after birth.

It is predominantly seasonal, preferring warm weather, occurring mostly in the summer and autumn months or year-round in tropical climates.

The virus itself is a single positive strand of RNA (Ribonucleic Acid – similar to the more commonly known DNA – but with some fundamental differences). The strand is enclosed in a protective coating called a capsid and can survive for up to two months outside the human body. Polio can't be caught from an animal or anything other than another person. Humans are the only natural source for the virus.

Entering through the mouth it follows the digestive tract. Latching onto the wall of the intestines the microbe uses the living cells of its host to multiply, eventually spreading to lymph nodes and entering the bloodstream. In approximately 95 per cent of the cases, the virus moves harmlessly with no effect through the body and is ultimately eliminated from the body in the feces.

Most affected persons feel a mild temporary effect, like a flu, as their bodies fight the virus. Others can develop stiffness in their backs or legs which will typically last from two to ten days before full recovery. But there is no lasting impact.

For the approximately one per cent whose nervous systems are attacked it can be catastrophic, resulting in permanent disability or death. There are three distinct types of the Polio virus – all are extremely virulent and produce identical symptoms

The virus invades the nervous system, destroying motor neurons – the nerve cells that control muscles. Paralysis results from Spinal Polio - which affects nerves in the spinal cord, attacking muscles in the legs but sometimes in the arms as well. Bulbar Polio, which attacks the brain stem, affects the swallowing, speaking and breathing muscles.

Between five and ten per cent of all people severely affected by Polio can die from asphyxiation.

Diagnosis is usually made from a stool sample or a swab of the pharynx (the cavity at the back of the nose and throat). Antibodies in the blood of infected patients can also be detected in the early stages. An increased white blood cell count and elevated protein in the spinal fluid is indicative of paralytic Polio.

The first recognized record of Polio is that of British novelist and poet Sir Walter Scott. He described his disease, contracted in 1773 at 18 months of age, very precisely and called it a severe teething fever which deprived him of the use of his right leg. His record was eventually influential in identifying Poliomyelitis as a disease.

British physician Michael Underwood wrote the first clinical description of Polio, calling it "a debility of the lower extremities" in 1795. Other clinical descriptions were made in Italy in 1813 and India in 1823.

It wasn't until 1840 that orthopedist Jakob Heine in Connstat, Germany, finally discovered and described what he labeled Infantile Paralysis – the first time the illness was recognized as a clinical entity. His work was followed up in 1890 by Swedish pediatrician Karl Medin, who published a study recognizing and describing Polio as an acute infection. Both men believed it to be bacterial in origin.

The name "Poliomyelitis", which means inflammation of the spinal cord, wasn't used until 1874.

One of Medin's students, Ivar Wickman, labeled it Heine-Medin Disease when he did the first clinical study of an epidemic, in Sweden in 1905, concluding that Polio was highly contagious. It was Wickman who identified the local school as having a prominent role in spreading the disease. In 1908 Austrian biologist Karl Lansteiner determined that Polio wasn't a bacterial infection at all, but a virus.

A virus is the smallest and simplest microbe in existence. Scientists knew viruses existed but no one ever actually saw one until the electron microscope was invented in 1930.

The first documented epidemics happened in Norway in 1868 and in Sweden during the 1880s. Small localized outbreaks at first but growing in intensity until, at its peak in the 1940 and 50s, Polio was paralyzing or killing a half million people worldwide every year.

The intensity of the publicity surrounding Polio made it the AIDs of its day, generating the same kind of dread that only an incurable, unpredictable disease of unknown origin can.

Nobody even knew what to call it. Dental Paralysis. Infantile Spinal Paralysis. Paralysis of the Morning. Regressive Paralysis. Essential Paralysis of Children.

The Toronto Star on August 17, 1910, called it a "Strange Epidemic", describing it as "An epidemic of poliomyelitis, or infantile paralysis, a comparatively new disease, which is attracting much interest among medical men the world over."

They didn't know when it would strike or where. All anyone knew for certain in the early years was that their children were at peril and there was really nothing they could do about it.

They would fall over without warning and never walk again. They would go to bed at night, healthy, and wake up in the morning unable to sit up, raise their head or swallow their own saliva. A simple test to determine whether a child possibly had Polio was to lay them face down on the floor and try to turn them over, looking for flaccid muscles in the legs.

Short of keeping them out of swimming pools, playgrounds, school, churches – any place people would gather – there were few things parents could do as a preventative. One man's grandmother wouldn't let him leave the house with hanging a cube of camphor – the smelly stuff in mothballs – around his neck to ward off the disease that had crippled so many children. He didn't get Polio but isn't convinced that it was due to the camphor.

People tried gargling with salt water, killing the family cat, scrubbing the toilet, bagging ashes from the stove, fumigating rooms with cyanide and reducing the amount of meat they ate. Nothing worked.

There was, and still is, no cure.

Treatment was an ongoing process that seemed to produce few results.

"I remember the treatment very well. There was a shot of penicillin every three hours for 16 days," recalls Polio survivor Dave Pritchard, "And there was this big red-haired matron named Nurse Mathers who came in, picked me up, took me across the hall, put me in a bathtub full of very, very hot water and put a sheet over the bathtub so only my head was sticking out."

A number of treatments were tried. Nerve grafting (grafting didn't work, but remaining nerves on the spine or the brain stem can develop new branches, called "Axons." The new nerves can reinvigorate muscles allowing modest recoveries of strength up to 18 months after infection). Electrotherapy. A nasal spray designed to block the virus from reaching the upper nasal nerves. Hitting the spine with wet towels to improve blood flow.

In the midst of such desperation some effective treatments were developed. An Australian nun, Sister Elizabeth Kenny, felt the prevailing treatment theory of the 1920s was inhumane. It suggested that totally immobilizing the victim with splints and plaster body casts during the convalescent stages of the disease was an effective means of preventing the shortening of muscles.

She advocated treating muscle spasms with hot, moist packs, shortened or paralyzed muscles with physiotherapy and early exercise to re-educate them. In 1940-41, Kenny travelled across Canada and the U.S. training nurses in her therapy – which is still used in the treatment of Polio survivors almost 70 years later.

The Iron Lung, a metal coffin-shaped air tight cylinder that symbolized both the worst of Polio and the best of medical technology at the time, was developed in 1928 at Children's Hospital in Boston, Massachusetts. The original model was powered by two vacuum cleaners and worked by changing the pressure inside the metal container to force air in and out of the patient's lungs.

For the first time victims of Bulbar Polio could be saved – but a single unit cost as much as the average house and there weren't enough of them (when the epidemic of 1937 hit Canada, there was only one Iron Lung in the entire country and it was already occupied. The Hospital for Sick Children in Toronto built 27 more units in their basement and shipped them out across the country. There were 1200 in the United States by 1959 – all of them in use).

Thousands of lives were saved by the Iron Lung, but the cost of treatment was prohibitive. Patients were encased in them for months or years. Sometimes for life. Iron Lungs were manufactured until the 1970s.

Public health authorities treated it like most other endemic diseases, associating it with poor hygiene, pollution, flies and poverty. They encouraged improved sanitation and quarantines. Parents had to show certificates proving their children didn't have Polio before they could enter or leave quarantined neighborhoods.

It became commonplace to find quarantine signs hanging on doors.

"Infantile Paralysis

Poliomyelitis

All persons not occupants of these premises are advised of the presence of Infantile Paralysis and are advised not to enter. The person having Infantile Paralysis must not leave the premises until the removal of this notice by an employee of the Department of Health."

It is strongly believed that prior to the twentieth century poor sanitation standards resulted in individual immunity systems being strong enough to combat the virus. Virtually everyone either had or was exposed to Polio but only the most severe cases were noticed.

Modern medicine, transportation accessibility and sanitation practices changed everything after the turn of the century.

As public health standards went up and sanitation improved, personal immunity decreased - making not just children, but also adults susceptible to the disease. Studies showed that improving child mortality rates corresponded with increasing incidents of Polio. Railroads and the advent of air travel made people more mobile than ever before and previously isolated areas, insulated from Polio, were no longer protected by their geography.

Likewise, the removal of geographical barriers enabled the disease to travel from areas where it had previously been contained.

Polio was never the killer painted in most imaginations. In 1952, during the worst epidemic in history, 58,000 victims were identified but only 3,145 people (including 1,873 children) died in the United States. That same year over 200,000 Americans died from Cancer, 30,000 were killed in accidents and 20,000 from Tuberculosis.

But it had the fear of the unknown, a history of hopes dashed because no solution had been found and there were no signs that one would be discovered soon. It had survivors who believed life held no future for them, with their withered limbs supported by heavy iron or steel posts with padded leather straps and lives confined to hospital wards full of Iron Lungs.

The epidemics seemed to come out of nowhere, striking almost every summer and affecting an ever increasing number of victims each time. Originally Polio had been considered an affliction of the poor – brought on by filth, poverty, overcrowding and ignorance. Then, as studies showed the poor actually had a lower incidence of Polio than those who lived in less crowded and cleaner neighborhoods, it became a middle class disease.

When Franklin Delano Roosevelt was diagnosed with Polio, it erased another so-called preventative - the myth that social privilege, wealth and age were barriers against infection.

He refused to admit he was permanently paralyzed and made it his life's mission to get better because he felt it essential to his political career. He taught himself, with the aid of iron braces and a crutch, to walk short distances by swiveling his torso in a manner that literally threw his legs out in front of him. In private he used an armless wheelchair but it was rarely seen in public.

Preferring to appear in public standing up he was supported on one side by an aide. Seated, his broad shoulders and thick neck made him appear larger than he was and drew attention from his legs, which were covered by a blanket.

In 1926 he built a cottage, which later became his "Little White House", in Warm Springs, Georgia, which he later developed into the Georgia Warm Springs Foundation – a hydrotherapy center for the treatment of Polio. Spring mineral water bubbled to the surface at a constant 86 degrees, summer and winter, making it a natural destination for people seeking therapy. Its mandate was eventually expanded to take care of patients with mobility issues of all types.

In 1945 it was renamed the Roosevelt Warm Springs Institute for Rehabilitation and today houses the World Polio Hall of Fame - dedicated to individuals who made a difference in the fight against Poliomyelitis.

After being elected President for his first term in 1933 FDR co-founded, in 1938 with Basil O'Connor, the National Foundation for Infantile Paralysis (NFIP), which focused on supporting research on Polio prevention and the rehabilitation of Polio victims.

Unlike most foundations, usually funded by wealthy families with their own philanthropic purpose, the NFIP was a non-partisan foundation where the bulk of the funds raised would come from the general public and the money would be aimed at finding a solution to one specific disease. It changed the nature of charitable foundations forever, attracting people by showing them they had a stake in the campaign and something to gain from their efforts – protection from disease.

The fund raising campaign was opened with a national radio appeal asking everyone in the nation to contribute a dime to fight Polio. Comedian Eddie Cantor is credited with giving the campaign its name – 'The March of Dimes.'

It motivated mothers across the country. Determined to protect their children they marched from door to door collecting the coins. Major Hollywood movie studios were persuaded to run a Polio documentary before their feature presentation and pass a March of Dimes box through the audience while it was showing. Towns competed to see which could collect the most money.

In Canada the government tried to fund Polio hospitalization policies and research through federal health grants. In 1948, they attempted to duplicate the American success by establishing the Canadian Foundation for Poliomyelitis (CFP). After struggling along for three years the CFP was restructured into provincial organizations, such as the Ontario March of Dimes, which expanded their mandate, as did the March of Dimes in the United States, to encompass research and treatment of all handicaps – no matter what the cause.

When Roosevelt died on April 12, 1945, the American dime was coincidently the only coin that didn't have a previous president's portrait printed on it. It was only suitable that his be the one.

Funds from the March of Dimes were used to fund Polio treatment centers across the United States, the Connaught Laboratories in Toronto, Ontario, and several researchers trying to unlock the secret to curing or preventing Polio. Among their number were two, Jonas Salk and Albert Sabin, who were soon to take their place in medical history.

I entered the 2006 Jacques Velneut Grand Prix at the Defi Sportif in Montreal, Quebec. It was my first opportunity to meet with and learn from top hand cyclists in Canada.

Where There's a Will

✦

Right from the beginning the media challenged Terry Fox – "Do you think you can do this because of your physical handicap?" You think they would have learned the answer when he gave it. Well, they didn't because they were asking me the same question almost 30 years later.

It wasn't just the media. It was family, friends and supporters. I had two years of people questioning my physically being able to complete the journey. A lot of people doubted we could even get on the road.

I hadn't hand cycled a single kilometer yet. I didn't even have a bike. This was a true pipedream. I never doubted I could do it. Just looking at the map, seeing the entire journey and deciding where each day would end. It didn't matter what happened, the days goal had to be achieved. If I completed each small step, I would achieve the journey. This wasn't as much about fulfilling a dream as it was about how I would now live my life.

I never saw it as a vacation. Never saw it as an opportunity to conquer the country. It was about getting the message out that we needed to take a part in stopping Polio. I needed to be clear about this being about education, rehabilitation and the eradication of the virus. For Terry, it was cancer. And not stopping until it was done.

Remembering what Matt had said to me at his wedding about calling Rotary, I talked to Kip Veale – she was a friend of my parents from their time in Whitehorse – and asked her what I should do. She suggested the same thing. So I called the president of the Whitehorse Rotary Club, Richard Buchan, and told him what I wanted to do and why. He listened very politely then told me, "We're all quite busy with our own projects so I don't think we're really interested."

I couldn't believe it. I was crushed. I sat on the idea for a couple of weeks thinking about it and I decided 'No. That can't be right.' But I wasn't sure what to do about it.

One night I went to pick up my mail. In Granger, the subdivision where I lived then, there is no mail delivery. Canada Post built this big shelter in which they put a bank of mail boxes where people would stop on their way home from work. Pam Buckway, a former territorial government Minister of Community Affairs and member of Rotary, and her sister Bev, who was eventually elected as Mayor of Whitehorse, were there checking their mail as well.

Pam asked me, "How did you make out with your project with the Rotary?"

Kip had told her about it.

"I talked to Richard and it really didn't seem to go anywhere." I expressed my frustration and told her I didn't think that could be right.

"Well, you know," Pam said, "If you're going to talk to anyone I think the person you should talk to is Allon Reddoch. He's been involved with Rotary's Polio Plus program for many years. And he has a medical background."

So I went home, called Allon, told him what I had in mind and asked "Can we sit down together?"

He said, "Sure."

When I met Allon in late 2005, I could see this glimmer in his eye. He knew this was a project to support and he believed strongly in it.

Later I found out while Allon was a medical student he worked in the Netherlands and encountered children with Polio in a village which was a Dutch Reform Church sect that didn't believe in immunization. This had been in 1972 when northern Europe had already been declared Polio free.

Later he travelled to Uganda and saw "crawlers" there also. When Rotary International started the Polio Plus program in 1985 he became very committed because he knew the need for ongoing immunization.

"It's all very well learning about it (Polio) from medical studies," he told me, "but when you see it first hand it makes a difference."

In our first meeting he explained to me that Polio Plus had mostly fallen off the Rotary radar because "when you don't see Polio, you don't think of Polio. In our society, there's heart and stroke and cancer – and everyone knows somebody who has been affected by one or the other. So it's at the top of your mind.

But when you've been doing a campaign for twenty years and you don't see the direct results it becomes difficult to maintain."

I had all sorts of goals for my journey. To raise money for Polio eradication. To build a museum of disability in Canada. To lobby the government to repeal the section of the immigration act that could have kept me out of the country. He was only interested in the Polio aspect – in particular the education part and the fundraising for Polio Plus and he convinced me to focus only on that.

After we had had several meetings he arranged for me to give a presentation to the Whitehorse Rotary Club.

When I gave the presentation a few of my friends and I had already come up with the name 'Cycle to Walk'. We'd talked a lot about it and decided it should be a three word title. We tried all sorts of suggestions but nothing seemed to work. It took weeks.

The name actually came to me while I was asleep. I woke up one night, about four in the morning, wrote down "Cycle to Walk" and went back to sleep. It was really weird.

By this time I also had a hand cycle coming.

In August, 2005, I was looking after my sister's house while she was away. One afternoon while watering the plants – at least that's what I tell my sister – a friend of theirs stopped by. Dev Hurlburt just wanted to eye up their driveway. Elisa's husband, Mike, does a lot of work for Dev without pay and Dev wanted to repay their generosity by paving their driveway.

He asked me how I was doing and what I was up to. We talked for a few minutes. Dev likes things to be blunt and straightforward because that's the way he is. I wanted to know if he had any ideas about how I might be able to go about getting started on this project.

So I just said to him, "You know, I'm thinking about hand cycling across Canada for Polio. This is my dream. I just need to find the resources to buy a hand cycle."

"Wow. That sounds like a really big project," he seemed very interested.

We talked about the idea a bit more and I outlined to him how I envisioned it working. "But the big issue is the bike. It's really expensive. It costs about six thousand dollars."

"It sounds like you really want to do this."

"Yeh I do."

Then, as he was leaving, he stopped and looked back at me.

"Just get it."

"Just get what?"

"The bike. Get it and send me the bill."

"Are you serious!? They're really expensive."

"Who are you dealing with?"

"James Black at Medichair Yukon."

"I'll talk to him. We'll get it done." Then he left.

I talked to James and told him "Dev's gonna pay for the bike." In the end Dev and James split the cost and we ordered this yellow 27-speed bike. It arrived in February, 2006.

It's funny. Mike and Elisa's driveway still isn't paved, but I got my bike.

I was able to go for my first hand cycle that spring. There was still a lot of ice and snow everywhere so I talked to the management at the Canada Games Centre. They agreed to let me use the indoor running/walking track for training.

When the first hand cycle arrived James and I headed up to the centre. It was quite exciting! Here I was up on the track on my new bike ready to go. Went around once. No problem. My confidence soared and I went a little faster. I hit the first sharp corner too fast, tipped and fell off the bike.

Cut my arm on the hard rubberized flooring and watched my bike smash into the wall. It's still got the dent in it to remind me. I was just lying on the track. James ran towards me. He looked pretty concerned. My first hand cycle lesson – don't go too fast on sharp corners - suddenly struck me as being incredibly funny.

"And I'm planning to go across the country on this thing?!" I laughed.

It was a challenge, not just for me, but for everyone involved. The people at Icycle Sport had never worked on a hand cycle before. Even my riding clothes were different from regular riding clothes. I didn't need the cushioned crotches or pockets in the back of the jerseys

I contacted Stephen Burke in Calgary - he's the head of the Canadian Paralympic Cycling Team, and used to live in the Yukon. He was thrilled with the plan and suggested I fly to Montreal for a hand cycling competition. This would enable me to learn more riding techniques and meet other hand cyclists.

Then I talked to Don White, who trains runners and skiers, and Mike McCann, a road cyclist at the senior level, about designing a training schedule.

To this point my personal journey had pretty much dictated to me that I had to go it by myself so once I got a hand cycle and set myself a goal, it didn't seem that much different. Cycling is a solitary challenge and I was all right with that. Climbing a hill at four kilometers an hour isn't that much different from walking alone to school.

At that time I was president of the Yukon Society Toward Accessible Recreation and Sport (YSTARS). The whole idea behind this group was to build inclusive communities using sport and recreation. I was coaching and teaching a wheelchair basketball program. Going into high schools and working with physical education students to teach them respect for people with long term mobility loss.

So, I thought, why don't we expand this program. We did a funding application for the Yukon Governments Community Development Fund

(CDF), and the first one failed because the CDF didn't see the need. The second one was approved and funds were made available for YSTARS to purchase six recreational hand cycles that would introduce Whitehorse residents to recreational hand cycling. Whitehorse was the first community in Canada to have a formal hand cycling program.

Following Stephen Burke's advice I entered the 2006 Jacques Velneut Grande Prix race at the Defi Sportif competition, which is held in Montreal every spring. I really shouldn't have been there. Here I was with the world's top hand cyclists and I didn't even have cycling shorts. I rode my first race in GAP cargo shorts!

On the night of the race the other athletes I met earlier in the day, and that I thought were going to support me, whizzed right by me as I was finishing my warm-up lap. As I crossed over the start line people yelled, cheered and clapped. I thought, "They're quite friendly here in Montreal. This is just great!"

I thought the race started at 7:30 so I pulled off the track to prepare. A lady ran across the track and asked me "Are you finished?"

"Finished?" I replied to her, "I haven't even started yet. The race starts at 7:30."

She smiled at me. "No. I'm sorry. The race started at 7:15." That explained why everyone just went whizzing by during my warm-up lap. They were actually racing.

So my first results in a hand cycle race say "Abandoned." As if I wasn't even there.

I made three presentations to Rotary, one of them to the Rotary Foundation District (which includes both the Yukon and Alaska members) dinner in February 2006, trying to sell them on my journey and Allon made one as well. In one of them I sat on the floor, then stood up and showed them how the braces and crutches changed the way I fit into society.

A lot of people were interested in what I had to say but I got the feeling that a lot of them didn't believe it would actually happen. Some initially said they wanted to be involved, then they backed out.

After one of the biggest presentations of my life where I opened up my entire life in the hopes they would support my dream, I was on a high. One member came up to me and said "You could have done a better job. You said a lot of 'ums'."

Then another person approached me and told me "I admire what you are doing but I won't support you unless you are a Rotarian."

You can imagine how I felt. Some of the most influential community members in one room, all of them successful in their businesses or jobs, and I had only worn shorts comfortably for two years.

After my second presentation to Rotary, Doug Ayers came up to me and told me he was interested in being part of the team. I don't think he really thought of it as being such a huge project. He said he could be part of the team and probably ride along with me on his bike every once in a while. At that time I was talking about riding down the Alaska Highway to start the journey and I think that was the part that really interested Doug.

It was at the 2006 Rotary Foundation District dinner, when I mentioned my concern about being able to come up with a road team that it truly started to come together. I think the fact that the Whitehorse Rotary Club had also arranged to bring the last Iron Lung left in the Yukon – it's in the museum in Mayo – to set up as a prop for my presentation really helped.

There were some Alaskan Rotarians there and they collected among themselves nine hundred dollars towards a hand cycle for the journey. Doug came up to me and firmly committed to being a part of a road team. I...and I don't think he...understood at the time just how much of an anchor that he and his wife Bertha were going to be for my ride. I know that Bertha definitely didn't. Apparently Doug didn't mention it to her until after he told me they were going.

"Why would you want to be part of this?" I asked him.

"I have been interested in Polio Plus since it started up," he told me, "And over the years that interest in Rotary has dropped. We, as Rotarians, didn't keep it in front of ourselves to work towards. The reason I would be involved with Cycle to Walk is because it's a perfect opportunity to make the eradication of Polio a live issue again. To get people interested again. To get Rotary back on track.

There are so many good issues in this world that it's hard to keep focused on one issue. And I see this as a way to get their attention again."

Allon was already committed and his influence started to attract others. Rotary has a lot of members from so many of society's communities. We needed to set up a non-profit society and a management board to organize the journey. There were permits to apply for that would allow me to cycle on the highways, accommodations to arrange, a website to build, sponsors to find and a myriad of other details that had to be taken care of before I could even start.

Audrey McLaughlin, who was the first woman to lead a federal political party in Canadian history, joined the board. She was leader of the New Democratic Party from 1989 to 1995. Since leaving politics she has worked in third world countries, knows the devastation of Polio in affected regions and has seen the immunization programs at work.

Valerie Royle, president of the Yukon Workers Compensation Health and Safety Board, came on board. She was originally asked by Allon to assist me in preparing a couple of powerpoint presentations. I realized pretty quickly that she had a strong background in communications, could help with sponsorship proposals and web development as well as assisting me with my public speaking skills.

Her husband Jaime also makes a mean cheesecake so there were plenty of good reasons to meet with Val in her dining room frequently.

We got a bank manager, Doug Janzen of the Bank of Nova Scotia, who would take care of the bank accounts and book keeping. Carmen Gibbons, the Director of Health Resources from the Kwanlin Dunn First Nation. Mal Malloch, a mediation consultant - he chaired the meetings. Lois Craig – an extraordinary volunteer. Bonnie Ross. Bob Lorimer – he's a professional engineer who specializes in project management. We even got someone from the federal prosecutor's office – Kate Brent, although we didn't need a prosecutor. She actually works in Human Resources.

I didn't know many of them very well when Cycle to Walk became a formal charity. It wasn't a perfect marriage because often my views clashed with theirs, but every one of them shared my view that we don't just live in houses, but in our communities and in the global village. All of them had given years of volunteer service in the Yukon and now they were going to give my project the benefit of their experience and knowledge.

I still hadn't given up on all the goals that I had when Allon first suggested that we focus on Polio education and eradication, so that had to be worked out.

I wanted to go in 2007. But they said, "We really need to reconsider this because we need more time to do more planning." So we put it off until 2008. Then they started talking about not going until 2009.

We worked on budgets – at one time it was estimated that it would cost us almost three quarters of a million dollars to make the trip. That wasn't going to happen. So we eliminated the "wants" and trimmed it down to the "needs." We would need two bikes. We would need a motor home to house the road crew and we would need another vehicle to pull the trailer with the extra bike, all the extra parts and the luggage in it.

Finally the board decided "We have to set a drop-dead date. If we don't have a specified amount of money in the bank by then, then we won't go." We were still hoping for a major corporate sponsor like Rick Hansen had for his Man in Motion world tour in 1985, but no one stepped forward and the deadline got closer without the money being there.

There was a night after we had a meeting and things hadn't gone so well that I went home, lay down on the floor and started to cry.

"Oh my gosh," I said to my room mate Jody Studney, "This board is never going to let me go."

Finally I made an appeal to them. I honestly believe I would have gone without them. I just decided I couldn't wait any longer. Some people still wanted to delay the trip for another year.

I told them ""I'm going. With or without you. There are people dying and becoming paralyzed right now due to the effects of Polio. This project can't get any better until Canadians actually see the effects that Polio can have on some one. And they're not going to buy into the program if I'm sitting up here in Whitehorse waiting for you to decide whether or not we can go."

Allon stayed true to his commitment. Even during the most challenging times he never wavered one bit. I've always said, "Thank you Allon" but he's always responded, "Don't thank me. I consider us partners in the forwarding of Polio eradication."

Doug and Bertha were always there for me. Bertha explained to me, "When we take something on we like to see it finished. Whatever we are interested in, any job we decide to undertake, we see it through to the end. We've always told our kids 'If you want to join something or be a part of something, then you're a part of it and we don't want to hear any whining that you don't want to go. It's a commitment you have so you complete it.' Once we're involved, we're committed.

Besides I've always wanted to drive across Canada. I just never thought I would be doing it at ten kilometers per hour."

When I asked her about Doug making the commitment before he talked to her, she just laughed.

"He does that," she said, "That's how we moved to the Yukon in the first place. We were living in Edmonton and Doug came home one day and told me we were moving to the Yukon because he and his business partner had decided to open an office in Whitehorse. He had never mentioned the Yukon and I had never heard of Whitehorse before that day. I said 'OK.' We packed up and headed north."

Doug told me that a former Rotarian, Murray Swales, stopped him on the street one day and told him that he heard about my journey, "Murray said to me 'I thought it had been done. What happened to the money we raised? What happened to all the work?' "

So the decision was made and a date selected – April 12, 2008.

There would be a ceremonial start in Whitehorse on April 10. We wouldn't ride down the Alaska Highway. It was too long a road and there's very little population along the way. For public exposure and fund raising, it's not a good highway to be on. The official start would be at Mile Zero on the TransCanada Highway in Victoria, B.C.

April 12 wasn't a random pick.

It was that day in 1980, that Terry Fox dipped his artificial leg in the Atlantic Ocean, at Cape Spear, Newfoundland, which was to be our end point, and started his cross-country run for cancer. I wanted to honor his memory.

Franklin Roosevelt died on April 12, 1945.

And April 12, 1955, was the day that Jonas Salk announced a vaccine had been discovered and tested that gave us better than a cure for Polio – it gave us a prevention.

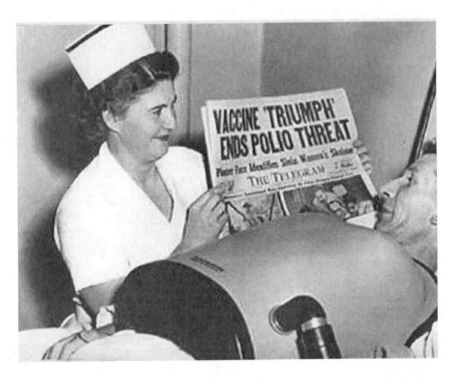

Newspapers, television and radio stations around the world trumpeted success of the Salk vaccine. It came too late for this man, confined to an Iron Lung, but it brought comfort to know that others would no longer be threatened by his fate.

The Great Race

✦

Scientists Race Time and Each Other to Find a solution to Polio

The most common misconception about Polio is that it's a vaccine to be taken, not a disease to be feared. It is that mistaken belief that keeps the virus at bay in the western world because it means that most people are willing to take the preventative – even if they don't understand why.

While two names, Jonas Salk and Albert Sabin, are most frequently associated with the development of vaccines in the 1950s the number of contributors - who brought them to their moments of glory - number in the hundreds and their achievements reach back over a century. Many of them weren't the leaders of their respective research teams and their names are lost to history. Others were simply overshadowed by those who attained the ultimate goal.

The Polio Hall of Fame is found on the outside wall of the Founder's Hall at the Roosevelt Warm Springs Institute for Rehabilitation in Warm Springs, Georgia. Unveiled in 1958, at a ceremony attended by Eleanor Roosevelt and almost all of the living scientists, the monument honors 17 people who played significant roles in the war against Polio. In 2008, four international organizations were added to the wall.

Bronze busts show sixteen men and one woman. Included are Polio pioneers Jakob Heine, Karl Medin, Ivar Wickman and Karl Landsteiner. Franklin Roosevelt and Basil O'Connor are also shown. The other eleven people commemorated on the wall are all American scientists, many

43

of whom received funding from the National Foundation for Infantile Paralysis (NFIP) and one of whom earned the Nobel Prize for Medicine while making invaluable contributions.

What is not shown on the wall is the fact that, although the honorees were from various cities and countries and some had no liking for others who are enshrined with them at Warm Springs, they had things in common.

A surprising number did not set out to conquer Polio. At first they did not even want to be doctors at all. Salk started his university career in pre-law, not pre-medicine. It was his mother who convinced him to change, telling him he would not be a very good lawyer. Sabin studied dentistry for three years before he decided he did not want to be one after all and switched to medical school.

John Enders got a business degree and initially made his living selling real estate. Unhappy with that career he studied languages with the idea of becoming a teacher. When teaching didn't work out either he turned to medicine.

The one quality that linked all of them was passion.

All of the Polio pioneers, enshrined in the Hall of Fame or not, started out hesitantly at first in their relationship with the disease but it soon held them irreversibly in it's grip.

Even though theirs was a field that demanded systematic, emotionless logic to achieve results, they were scientific romantics, lured by a dream of an imaginary world where anything – even a vaccine for Polio – was possible. Eventually they were all lulled by some gravitational force toward the greater cause, ultimately finding themselves deeply stirred by the realization that their place in the affairs of the world would be measured by the effect they had on the fate of individual lives.

Discoveries in science depend upon logical deductions based upon well-established general principles or theories, which must then be experimentally corroborated. Medical research is not so cut and dried.

It is an uncertain science where complex and obscure questions are studied and experimental ideas do not nessecarily emerge from vague concepts. Researchers in medicine need to act somewhat more randomly. They take more calculated risks without endangering the general population, in the hope that they will see some unexpected result which may further future research.

Until Karl Landsteiner determined in 1908 that Poliomyelitis was a virus, not a bacterial infection, researchers had been heading in the wrong direction. Viruses need living cells in which to thrive and, since the process of developing tissue cultures was still unknown, a living host was required to study the virus. Landsteiner had made his discovery injecting spinal cord tissue into monkeys.

It wasn't until 1926 that Thomas Rivers, from the Rockefeller Institute for Medical Research in New York City and considered the father of modern virology, determined reproduction of viruses depends entirely upon living cells of a host.

As the epidemics started to become more frequent, increasingly widespread and greater in the numbers of people affected, the scientists had more information and subjects to study. They were also under a massive amount of public pressure. Children were paralyzed and dying even as the researchers worked.

The NFIP revolutionized the way charities raised funds and made available to Polio researchers funds that were not obtainable in other areas of medical study or in other countries. Millions of dollars were spent setting up virology programs and Polio units across the United States. The first grant went to the Yale School of Medicine in 1936. Some funds were invested into units and programs in Canada, but the NFIP did so quietly in partnership with Canadian Life Insurance companies.

It was universally agreed that the best way to stop Polio was to prevent it. The only way to do that was to develop a vaccine.

But no progress could be made until researchers determined how many strains of Polio there were and how the disease was spread. Without that information early attempts to generate a vaccine failed.

In 1936 a research assistant at New York University, Maurice Brodie, was able to produce a small amount of a formaldehyde-killed Polio vaccine. A test of three thousand children produced allergic reactions, but no immunity. A pathologist from Philadelphia, John Kollmer, claimed to develop a vaccine that same year. His test group also produced no immunity and he was blamed for actually causing a number of cases. These failures haunted future field tests for years afterward.

Physician Charles Armstrong, working in the Hygienic Laboratory for the U.S. Public Health Service in Ohio, was able to transmit a rare and mild type of Polio virus from monkeys to cotton rats, then to white mice in 1939. This encouraged scientists to adapt innovative, more imaginative methods of research. It also started Armstrong on a track to develop a nasal spray vaccine, which he self-tested before abandoning it.

Nasal sprays had already been used with no controls in the southern United States and Western Canada in 1936. A control test was conducted in Toronto, Ontario, in 1937 which demonstrated that particular spray was not only ineffective, it also caused permanent damage to the sense of smell in some subjects.

David Bodian and Howard Howe, at John Hopkins University in Baltimore, Maryland, finally narrowed 196 different tested strains down to only three distinct types. In the meantime other researchers had been independently finding pieces of the puzzle.

45

The virus had been isolated from the human gastrointestinal tract and sewage waters, pulling the medical community from their laboratories into the field. They started trapping biting insects, testing sewage and drawing blood from victims to find how it was transmitted from one person to another.

Bodian's co-worker, virologist Isabel Morgan, is the only woman in the Hall of Fame. In 1944 she injected inactive vaccine into monkeys which, following the inoculation, developed an immunity to high concentrations of the Polio virus. It was the first time the concept of using anything other than a live virus had been tried. Only Morgan's reluctance to use the vaccine in human testing, then her decision to leave research medicine and get married, prevented it from being used in the 1940s.

John Paul and Joseph Melnick from Yale University in New Haven Connecticut, used a rare outbreak of Polio among the Inuit people in Canada's high Arctic in 1948 to explore the reasons behind apparent adult immunity and the role of antibodies in blocking the disease. They compared that study to one they conducted in Cairo, Egypt, where there was evidence of widespread infection combined with few actual outbreaks. The two were able to determine how the virus was transmitted and proposed public health standards for possibly immunizing a population that did not have a vaccine.

The stage was now set to resolve the next problem – how to harvest the Poliovirus safely and in sufficient volumes for research to be conducted.

A short paper published in 'Science' journal by three researchers in 1949 not only answered the question, it earned them the 1954 Nobel Prize for Medicine.

The principles of cultivating bacteria to develop vaccines and drugs were established in the 1870s by Robert Koch – who won the 1905 Nobel Prize for Medicine. However viruses proved to be much more resistant to the concept. Unlike bacteria, viruses are incapable of growing in artificial lifeless cultures. In a test tube a virus simply becomes an inert chemical substance. Only in the interior of living cells can it multiply.

Virologists had been reduced to inoculating animals, observing their reactions and trying to make deductions about the nature of the infection based upon mildly contaminated properties. They were viable for too short a time to be of any value

John Enders and Thomas Weller from Harvard University's Research Division of Infectious Disease in Boston, Massachusetts, and Fred Robbins from Western Reserve University in Cleveland, Ohio, used the same technique, but used human embryonic tissue (stem cells) for the culture. They were able to isolate the virus from the specimen. The ability to separate the virus from the tissue for study provided virologists with the ability to accumulate a safe reservoir of uncontaminated Poliovirus which, in turn, made possible the mass production of a vaccine.

The only obstacle left was figuring out how the virus reached the brain stem or spinal column. It had long been speculated by researchers that Polio entered the body through the mouth and worked its way down the digestive tract. But no one had yet been able to figure out how it got from there to the nervous system.

In 1943 Yale researcher Dorothy Horstmann, confused by the fact that blood drawn from Polio test subjects always tested negative for the virus, wondered if it could only be detected in the blood before the infection actually reached the nervous system. She injected the virus into monkeys, tested their blood immediately after injection and again after it affected their nervous system – confirming her theory. Her study, published in 1952, suggested that antibodies in the blood stream could potentially block the disease. David Bodian later confirmed Horstmann's results in an independent test.

There were three distinctively different approaches to the development of a Polio preventative.

The original, more universal approach taken was to find a live oral Polio vaccine (OPV). The live vaccine approach had certain theoretical advantages. It multiplied in the digestive tract, as did the Polio virus, and spread through the body as if it were an actual infection – effectively filling the gaps the wild virus would normally exploit. It was also easy to administer, only one dose was required, immunity was almost instantaneous and lasted a lifetime.

The number of virologists pursuing the OPV included two transplanted Poles living in the United States, Hilary Koprowski, working at the Lederle Laboratories in New York and Albert Sabin, the head of Pediatric Research at the University of Cincinnati in Cincinnati, Ohio.

Jonas Salk, at the University of Pittsburgh in Pittsburgh, Pennsylvania, previously had success with an inactivated influenza vaccine so his experience suggested that an inactivated Polio virus (IPV) might be the answer. He also drew on the IPV work conducted by Isabel Morgan in 1944.

IPVs were administered by booster shots and would only provide immunization for a limited period. The shots would have to be retaken every few years.

Salk's academic rival at the University of Pittsburgh, William Hammon, was opposed to the use of vaccines, calling them risky, costly and inefficient. He advocated passive immunization with gamma globulin - the fraction of blood that contains antibodies against Polio. Studies had shown that human gamma globulin could protect monkeys against the virus.

Koprowski developed an OPV in 1950 and started running relatively successful field trials in countries outside of the United States and Canada. It was the first time in world history that Polio had been prevented by a vaccine but because the trials were being conducted outside of the Polio hotbed of North America, the accomplishment was essentially unrecognized. The field study was tainted by the fact that his vaccine not only prevented Polio in some test subjects, it actually caused it in others.

He also provided samples of his vaccine to Sabin – a professional courtesy that would later become a bone of contention between the two.

Sabin announced in 1953 that he had isolated avirulent strains of Polio and started a small test program with himself, his family and eighty prison inmates who volunteered to take part in 1955.

Hammon was the first to go to the American public for a test, injecting 54,000 children in Utah, Texas, Iowa and Nebraska during the 1951-52 epidemic. He used a "double-blind, placebo-controlled" clinical trial – one of the first times the accepted current standard method of conducting medical trials was ever used. Some participant received the gamma globulin and others received a placebo. Neither the recipients nor the researchers would know who received which until the trial was completed.

Final results determined that the incident of paralytic Polio in the gamma globulin group was less than half of that in the placebo group. It was a success but gamma globulin was expensive and in short supply. During the 1953 epidemic public health authorities concluded mass inoculations were ineffective because there wasn't enough in existence and most were receiving the shots too late to be of any use.

At the same time that Hammon was running his trial, the team headed by Salk was getting ready for their first IPV safety tests. The Pittsburgh group had come up with an experimental vaccine containing a "killed" or inactivated virus which could trigger immunity.

The first tests were conducted in 1952 on paralyzed Polio patients at the D.T. Watson Home for Crippled Children in the borough of Leetsdale, Pennsylvania and the Polk State School. The idea was to use children who already had antibodies in their system because they had already been affected. It meant the children couldn't be hurt by the vaccine but if it increased their antibody levels the researchers would have evidence it worked.

In May 1953, Salk began a community-based trial. Almost 700 children, including his own, were involved in the test where the vaccine was administered, preceded and followed by blood tests to check antibody levels.

Word of the vaccine started to circulate and in the wake of the 1952 epidemic the pressure to speed up development was intense, but Salk had a problem. He didn't have the capability to develop the 3,000 litres of vaccine needed to conduct a widespread clinical test.

The National Foundation for Infantile Paralysis had quietly been funding the Connaught Medical Research Laboratories at the University of Toronto in Toronto, Ontario, for a number of years.

In 1949 three scientists at Connaught, Joseph Morgan, Helen Morton and Raymond Parker, developed a chemically pure synthetic culture, called Medium 199, in which Polio viruses rapidly multiplied. NFIP turned to researcher Leone Farrell, who had developed "the Toronto Technique," a unique method of gently rocking large bottle containing bacteria to stimulate growth, to figure out how to produce the virus in bulk quantities.

Farrell made a simple adjustment to her system, rocking the bottles full of Medium 199 in incubator rooms warmed to body temperature. The result was an abundance of live Poliovirus.

For months prior to the trial, bottles of live virus were packed into ice, placed inside dairy cans and loaded into the back of a station wagon parked at the loading bay of Connaught. The cargo was then driven across the border to the United States twice a week on their way to two American pharmaceutical companies, Parke Davis in Detroit, Michigan, and Elli Lilly in Indianapolis, Indiana, where the virus was then "killed."

The Francis Field Trial, headed by Thomas Francis, director of the University of Michigan Poliomyelitis Vaccine Evaluation Center, and launched in April, 1954, was the largest medical experiment in history. One point eight million children, called Polio Pioneers, in 44 states and three Canadian provinces were involved in the "double blind, placebo-controlled" test. About 440,000 actually got the vaccine. Another 220,000 were injected with the placebo, Medium 199, and the rest were given nothing at all – they were simply observed as part of the control group to see if any contracted Polio.

With pictures of the 1953 epidemic still depressingly fresh in the public memory, attention was riveted on the test. A Gallup poll found that more Americans knew about the Polio trials than knew the full name of the President of the United States – Dwight David Eisenhower.

On April 12, 1955, the announcement was made by Francis during a press conference held in Ann Arbor, Michigan. Television, radio and newspaper headlines around the world shouted it out – Salk's vaccine was effective and safe. Within days of the announcement, six pharmaceutical companies in the United States started producing the vaccine. Connaught Laboratories had already started tests in Canada with their own version on April 1, 1955.

The specter of failed vaccine tests in the 1930s came back to haunt them before the end of the month. In the rush to produce Salk's vaccine, U.S. health officials let batches slip through without testing. One batch, produced by Cutter Laboratories in California, resulted in 79 previously unaffected children contracting paralytic Polio.

The U.S. promptly temporarily ceased all production until it was determined the problem was limited to a few lots from the one company. In Canada the government under Louis Saint-Laurent wanted to follow the American lead and suspend the program. Minister of Health and Welfare, Paul Martin, Sr., himself a Polio survivor who had watched his son wrestle with the same disease in 1946, took it upon himself to champion the cause and authorized the continuation of the immunization program.

By the end of the year, ten million children in five countries had been immunized. Incidents of Polio in the U.S., which in 1954 numbered over 38,000, dropped to only 2,525 by 1960.

Salk never patented his vaccine. He wanted it to be universally available, not limited to those who could afford it. When asked during an interview "Who owns the patent on this vaccine?" the bespectacled scientist looked confused.

"There is no patent," he responded, "Could you patent the sun?"

In Cincinnati, Albert Sabin was still quietly working on an OPV, which he still insisted would be superior to the IPV. In 1957 he was ready for larger clinical trials but the United States was in no rush to host the test. Sabin ran his clinical trials through the World Health Organization in the Soviet Union, Holland, Mexico, Chile, Sweden and Japan.

The results were outstanding. The OPV was inexpensive, easy to administer and appeared to have the ability to spread, much like Polio itself, beyond recipients who had not received the vaccine at all. It also proved to be effective with adults whereas the Salk vaccine had limited success with older recipients.

Medical authorities in the Soviet Union were so impressed they eventually inoculated their entire population with Sabin's OPV, then offered to give it away it to any country that wanted it.

Once the safety of the Sabin vaccine had been established internationally, the United States permitted trials starting on 'Sabin Sunday', April 24, 1960. They licensed the vaccine in 1961. While Salk's IPV had reduced the incidence to Polio to a fraction of what it was in the early 1950s, Sabin's OPV completely eliminated the wild Polio virus everywhere it was used.

There were drawbacks. Public health officials conceded that some children – about one in a million – may have developed Polio because of the vaccine. Sabin and Koprowski never conceded that live vaccines might be responsible.

In 2008 a Staten Island, New York, man, apparently stricken with Polio after changing his daughter's diaper in 1979, successfully argued in court that an OPV passed through her digestive system and infected him. The decision is being appealed.

Unfortunately, success brought out the worst in everyone involved. Now that the goal had been attained, the researchers turned their attention on each other and they really didn't like each other all that much.

The public saw only the rancor that Sabin held towards Salk. Sabin had long been a critic of the IPV, lobbying strongly against it in the early 1950s and obviously was embittered that Salk had beaten him to the finish line. During a medical conference in Copenhagen in 1960 he turned to Salk and stated simply that he was "out to kill the killed-virus."

"Salk didn't discover anything," growled Sabin in an interview in later years, calling the killed-virus preparation "pure kitchen chemistry."

While Salk was the public hero, winning civilian awards including the Congressional Gold Medal in 1955 and the Presidential Medal of Freedom in 1977, he was denied admission to the National Academy of Sciences apparently because of the influence of Sabin, who was a long-time member.

Sabin wasn't without his own detractors. Koprowski complained that the vaccine delivered by Sabin had actually been discovered by him and Sabin had only gotten it because he (Koprowski) had given it to him – along with the questions about its safety.

The real resentment against Salk came not from his competitors, but from his colleagues. It began with the first press conference on April 12, 1955, when he failed to mention his co-workers at the University of Pittsburgh. It continued during an interview with CBS newsman Edward Murrow.

When Murrow asked who else had contributed to the Polio vaccine, Salk cited the inventor of the hypodermic syringe and no one else. When photographed for the cover of 'Time' magazine in 1954, he was alone – sharing fame with none of his team, instead being illustrated with five syringes.

Patiently silent at first, his colleagues eventually publicly admitted being resentful of Salk for being excluded. Years later in a newspaper interview Salk acknowledged his failure to include his colleagues.

"Perhaps a more conscious attempt might have been made," he said, "and perhaps should have been made to lists the names of each individual more prominently rather than, as was implied, that the satisfaction came from the work itself."

Connaught Laboratories, also nudged aside in the Salk star-making campaign, had just started to make its impact in the worldwide war against Polio. Vaccine manufactured in the United States couldn't be exported without meeting domestic standards, established in 1960, and federal licensing.

Connaught, located in Canada, could export its IPV and OPV vaccines to any country that wanted it. Canadian manufacturers didn't require an export permit and, as long as the vaccine met World Health Organization standards, the exported product only had to satisfy the requirements of the importing country.

The U.S. regulations made the Connaught Medical Research Laboratories the largest supplier of Polio vaccines to the world by 1962. Connaught continues its research and manufacturing of vaccine even though it has gone through various owners over the years, ultimately ending up as the Canadian component of Sanofi-Pasteur, the global vaccine arm of France's pharmaceutical giant Sanofi-Aventis.

In 2005, a new vaccine against Polio was developed by Sanofi-Pasteur and successfully tested in northern India. It was the first new OPV developed since the Sabin vaccine.

I was accompanied by teachers and students from several schools when Cycle to Walk started on April 10, 2008, with a ceremonial ride in Whitehorse, Yukon.

You must be the Change

✦

The Wednesday night before our April 10, 2008, Whitehorse start I had dinner with my sisters Rani and Elisa, my brother-in-law Mike and niece and nephew Kaitlyn and Christian. Then I needed time for myself and went for a walk along the Yukon River.

I thought about how fortunate I was to have been given the opportunities I've had in life. About the three years it took for Cycle to Walk to become a reality. Endless emails, endless meetings, hundreds of laps in the swimming pool and thousands of kilometers cycling along the Alaska Highway. Now it was only 24 hours from actually starting.

Most people I know who run or cycle for a cause are usually doing it for something that people recognize and can relate to. The child in their neighborhood who needs a kidney. Someone who's fighting cancer. They cycle for the planet. They swim for the whales. Or they run for those who can't.

We do it because it's personal and we know our efforts will be rewarded when we improve the lives of others. It isn't right for people to spend every day dreading tomorrow. How do you measure that?

I thought about my hand cycle and how it changed my life. My world had been pretty much confined to where I could go and what I could do with a brace and crutches. That was a lot, but the hand cycle opened up a whole new world of trails and experiences for me. And now maybe I could use it to do the same for someone else.

Polio was a bit of a reach for most Canadians. It's personal for me but they didn't know anything about it. This wasn't going to be easy – either physically or otherwise. But I thought we had done a good job of getting ready to educate them. It's hard to judge the value of a cross Canada trek. We would encounter a large number of people and hopefully generate some publicity, but most donors to any cause usually seek a long term relationship with the organization or charity they are going to support. Canadians don't have any such relationship with Polio unless they are Rotarians, have seen or experienced the effects.

The board agreed we needed someone with the road crew to keep on top of the media relations early in the trip so we offered a three-week placement through Shirley Muir, who teaches a Communications and Media Relations course at Red River Community College in Winnipeg, Manitoba.

We contacted her following a trip I made to Old Crow, the Yukon's northernmost community, to teach wheelchair basketball and talk to them about community inclusion for those with limited mobility. CBC radio journalist, Sandy Coleman, was in Old Crow and did a report on my trip. I talked to her about Cycle to Walk and she suggested the board ask Shirley to help develop a media strategy.

Shirley, Sandy told me, would be a great resource because she worked on media for Terry Fox when he ran his Marathon of Hope. During one of our discussions Shirley mentioned she was looking for a practicum for some of her students.

Two of her students applied for the placement and Chris Madden was one of them.

I'm sure he truly believed his practicum would last only three weeks, but at the end of that time we felt we couldn't do without him. So his contract was extended to the finish. His A-plus academic efforts spilled over onto the road and bolstered the campaign in many ways from media relations to updating the website, photography and creating public speaking notes for myself.

The road crew that would accompany me across the entire country was small in numbers – Doug and Bertha Ayers and Chris Madden, but dedicated. On the banks of the Yukon that night, I thought about anthropologist Margaret Mead and what she once said.

"Never doubt that a small group of thoughtful, committed citizens can change the world. Indeed it is the only thing that ever has."

The previous Saturday a fund raising 'Evening of Music' was held at Whitehorse United Church where a number of talented musicians, led by Barry Kitchen, shared their gift of music for Cycle to Walk. The place was packed and we took the opportunity to introduce the road team and show people the "Purple Pinky Project."

In third world countries, when a child is inoculated, their pinky finger is usually dipped in a purple dye. The color tells other people doing the inoculations this particular person has already received their dose. We weren't giving vaccine, but donors had their pinky dipped in the dye.

That same night there was another evening of music fund raiser across the country at St. Luke's Anglican Cathedral in Sault Ste. Marie by Stephen Mallinger, an Ontario musician. I found it amazing that the word was already spreading.

The days leading up to our April 10 ceremonial start in Whitehorse were busy. I was interviewed on radio and for the newspapers. Gave speeches to Rotary clubs. There was a photo opportunity with Alex Furlong, president of the Yukon Federation of Labour, as they presented Cycle to Walk with an eight thousand dollar donation. Kim Farrell and Jerry Quaile, the owners of M&M Meats hosted a barbeque where we sold hamburgers and T-shirts as well as received donations.

One of the disagreements that had been discussed in board meetings was school visits. I wanted to cram in as many as possible. Some board members opposed me speaking in schools since they felt my immune system left me vulnerable to all the "school germs." I gave a couple of talks before leaving Whitehorse including one to the students at Grey Mountain Primary – which was the first school I ever attended.

One thing I hadn't thought of. I had to take time to shave. Heavy snow that winter had forced me to go south to Vancouver for two months to train on the hand cycle. While there I grew a beard. When I returned Shelley Williamson, the executive director for Cycle to Walk, took one look at my goatee and said "That's going to be coming off your face."

She reminded me of my high school days when my Mom would tell me that my goatee always made me look like a thug or that I had a rat on my face.

The morning of the day I had dinner with my family and went for my walk along the river, the Yukon Legislature recognized Cycle to Walk on the floor of the house. Then I spent the afternoon going around town saying good-bye to my former colleagues and my friends. I didn't ask them if they were glad to see me go, knowing that it meant they wouldn't have to listen any more to daily updates about Cycle to Walk, my frustrations and my dreams.

Doug and Bertha, committed to being the road team managers for the entire six months, had already headed down to Victoria to prepare for the official start on Saturday. Doug had shut down his business for the duration and Bertha took early retirement from her job at the Department of Education. I was totally overwhelmed by what they had already given to my dream and we hadn't even started yet!

Allon and Mary (Reddoch) had also headed south along with Shelley (Williamson).

Standing there, watching the water boil along in the open channel in the ice, it occurred to me that I had to leave tomorrow also, right after our official launch here in Whitehorse. Then I remembered I hadn't finished packing yet. So I cut off my walk and headed home.

No matter how hard I try, I can't capture words that could truly describe my emotions on the morning of Thursday, April 10. I felt so proud to be a Yukoner. The community had done so much to encourage me while I was getting ready.

I went to the bus depot to pick up some parcels and the guy behind the counter handed me a donation. While training on the highway, there were so many honks from drivers and people waving. When I went into the local coffee shops people constantly wished me well and asked how they could donate or take part.

A couple of days earlier I went to a Rotary luncheon and I don't think I even heard the guest speaker. I just kept looking around and thinking that without the people in this room, none of this would have happened.

I was excited. I was scared. I knew that when I took the next step, there was no turning back.

It was still cold in the mornings – it may have been spring but winter didn't seem to want to let go. The shoulders of the road had snow drifts on them and there was a cold wind coming out of the north.

Cathy Foster, the woman who now owns 41 Firth Road - the house where I learned how to walk, let us start in her home. Rani, Elisa, Mike, Kaitlyn and Christian were with me. My sisters and I talked about growing up in the house. I reminded them of how I threw myself head first down the stairs just for fun and scared our parents to death in the process. Cathy showed me my old bedroom. Then it was time to stop reminiscing and take the first step in Cycle to Walk. I took a deep breath, thanked God for everything in my life and we walked out.

We went out the front door, just like we did when we were kids and we walked down the driveway and onto the street. There was a small group waiting there that included a number of people who had known me as a kid. My grade one teacher was there! We walked down Firth Road to my hand cycle that was parked beside the fire hydrant I used to walk to - about 50 meters in total.

I had to say something so I held up the first leg brace I had ever had. It's pretty tiny. It took on a living existence of its very own for the next six months. Bertha named it "Little Brace." "Where's Little Brace?" "We need Little Brace." It was another person on the road with us.

I almost couldn't speak. I was choking back tears and trying to find words.

"I just walked from my house at 41 Firth. The house where I first learned to walk. The brace I carried in my hand was the first brace I ever used. The walk to this fire hydrant, which today took me about two minutes, used to take me 45 minutes."

Then I handed my crutches and Little Brace to my sister, sat down on the hand cycle and started to pedal. The RCMP had an escort car to lead me and Rani drove my car behind me. I rode to Grey Mountain Primary School, which is just down the street and there was a huge crowd there. A lot of them were kids and they carried signs and I could hear them cheering "Go Ferris! Go Ferris!" When we went up Lewes Boulevard, every student and staff from Christ the King Elementary School were there clapping and cheering.

I stopped at the legislative building and the Midnight Sun Pipe Band piped me into the building. There was a ceremony with the Premier, Dennis Fentie, some of his ministers and a lot of other people as well.

Bev Buckway, she was mayor of Whitehorse by now, remembered our conversation at the mailboxes. She told me Cycle to Walk was "the most geographically challenging effort to eradicate Polio that we will see in our time. Like all national events, it starts with the dream of one person."

Alex Furlong told me he would be at Cape Spear when I got there.

At the end of the ceremony I got back on the hand cycle and did what I knew I was going to be spending most of the next few months doing - I rode up a long hill. Robert Service Way from the legislative building to the airport.

There were dozens of kids from Grey Mountain Primary, Vanier School and the Wood Street School riding with me. I was honored to share the road with so many people and children. I was overjoyed to share this kind of a day, this particular day, with my community.

I had one more official start to my journey to go through, in Victoria, at Mile Zero of the TransCanada Highway, on Saturday, and I knew it was going to get pretty lonely because it was just going to be me and the road team from then on.

The day reminded me of what Dr. Jonas Salk once said about why he and the other researchers persisted with their efforts.

"Hope lies in dreams, in imagination, and in the courage of those who dare to make dreams into reality."

My dream lay behind me now. My reality was the next 7,140 kilometers in front of me.

The Ferris Family at Mile Zero of the TransCanada Highway on April 12, 2008. (L to R) Mom, Matthew, Jenny and Clipper, Rani, me, Mattie, Elisa, Jill and Ellie, Dad.

One Hand Crank at a Time

✦

We all woke up early on Saturday morning because, as Bertha said, "this is the start of something big."

The Friday had been busy. Doug, Bertha and Lynne Morris, my godmother, who came down from Whitehorse to join the road crew through B.C. and Alberta, were busy getting the vehicles ready. We had a 24-foot motor home, which was sleeping quarters for the road crew when we didn't have billets or donated hotel rooms.

I was actually going to be able to sleep in a hotel room or in a billet's house every night because I needed the bathtub to clean up in – I can't take a shower because I can't stand up without my brace and it has parts that might rust if they get wet too often.

There was also a Suburban pulling a trailer in which we stored the spare bike, all the T-shirts and spare parts and our suitcases. I even had a sports coat and dress pants hanging in there.

Chris kept taking me from media interview to media interview. We got great coverage from the Victoria Times Colonist and Patricia Wade Designs had really promoted and advertised Cycle to Walk throughout the entire city – everyone seemed to know it was happening.

Later in the afternoon we had a walk through of the events that were going to happen next day at Mile Zero in Beacon Hill Park. My brother Matt surprised me! He'd flown from New Zealand to share in the launch. My entire Canadian family was there. I was overwhelmed. It meant so much to me.

The Rotary Club of Victoria hosted a dinner for Cycle to Walk, then it was time to go to bed. But I couldn't sleep, I was excited, scared, happy. I felt so ready to start. It was time. My dream was four years old. I, and Allon, and dozens of others had put in hundreds of volunteer hours working towards this one day for three years. My training had consisted of 3,000 kilometers of hand cycling and 10,000 very repetitive lengths of a 25-meter swimming pool.

For me, that night wasn't about sleep. It was time to start waking people up.

We started Saturday morning with a small private ceremony - just myself, the road crew, a few friends and my family. We went to Clover Point. I know I spoke to them but I can't remember what I said. The important part was dipping "Little Brace" in the Pacific Ocean three times – once each for Polio eradication, education and rehabilitation. Then everyone else did the same thing.

My Dad said a blessing over the road team. For me, that was when the journey truly began.

I climbed onto my hand cycle and set off for Mile Zero where the official launch ceremonies would take place. They were quite different from the quiet contemplation of our small gathering at Clover Point.

A marimba band provided the entertainment and there was a pretty big crowd of Victoria Rotarians, some Polio survivors and former Yukoners.

"I did not hesitate because his cause is pure," Yukon commissioner (territorial equivalent to provincial lieutenant governor) Geraldine Van Bibber, Cycle to Walk's honorary chairperson, told the crowd assembled at the start in Victoria, "What is he giving? Himself. Ramesh not only inspires, but allows hope to filter through. The hope is that Polio can be beaten – one child, one country at a time."

Our member of parliament Larry Bagnell also spoke. He is one of the most supportive people I have ever known. He and his wife Melissa seem to be everywhere and involved in everything. His work ahead of us as we travelled east during Cycle to Walk was nothing short of amazing.

"I am confident that Cycle to Walk will make a tremendous positive difference in the lives of Canadians as well as the citizens of the world who have been impacted by Polio." Then he gave me a bouquet of orange lilies.

BRITISH COLUMBIA

April 12 - April 30, 2008

As I prepared to get onto the hand cycle Jenny suddenly blurted out "Ramesh! I'm so worried!"

"Not to worry," I replied with a bravado I'm not sure I really felt myself, "We have a risk management plan." Then I swung down onto the bike.

A banner was stretched across the roadway, held at each end by children, Boy Scouts and Polio survivors. I rode right through the middle of it. There were a group of bike riders including two former Yukoners, Justine and Katherine Scheck, accompanying me.

We made one stop about an hour after starting. At a store called The Country Grocer where the owner wanted to present us with a donation and the local Rotary club was holding an outdoor barbeque – it was a beautiful sunny, warm day. They had a high school band playing and everyone seemed so festive. What a great way to begin the journey!

Then it was a short ride down the Lochside Trail to the B.C. Ferries terminal where they let me ride my hand cycle onto the ferry and made a public announcement to the passengers about Cycle to Walk.

When we disembarked just south of the city of Vancouver on the other side of the Strait of Georgia from Victoria, we cycled a short distance towards Ladner, B.C., then stopped. Doug painted a small orange mark on the pavement and stuck a flag in the dirt on the shoulder of the road. Tomorrow, when we started again, we would line the front tire up with the mark or flag. The entire route was being mapped by Global Positioning System (GPS). This insistence on detail meant we couldn't cheat by starting ahead of where we stopped each night or it would show up as a gap in the line on the website map.

In fact, there are a couple of gaps on the map. Once when the GPS unit didn't work for awhile and another time when we weren't permitted to travel on a portion of the highway for safety reasons. To compensate for the part we couldn't ride I rode circles around a parking lot until we covered the nessecary distance. It made for a pretty weird entry on the GPS map, but it also meant we didn't miss a single kilometer in the entire trip. We marked and flagged the road at the end of every cycling day for the rest of the trip.

That night I found myself sitting on the lawn in front of our hotel, wearing a head lamp and digging through one of my bags. I realized I severely over-packed for this journey and sent back a suitcase or hockey bag full of stuff from different places all the way across the country. This time I was searching for my Play Station Video Game. I don't know what I was thinking when I packed it, but I actually thought I would have time to play on it. Between cycling and blogging every day it made the entire journey without ever being used.

Chris was outstanding at getting the attention of media. Before we finished crossing the country I talked to over 200 different media people on radio, television and in newspapers. That's more than one interview every day. There were days when I didn't do any interviews. There were days when it seemed like I didn't do anything else. The first day in Victoria had several and we spent an entire day with the press in Vancouver on the second one.

The only media that Chris never made any headway with was the national news bureau of the Canadian Broadcasting Corporation (CBC). They kept telling him "If we do one, we have to do them all." We never really bought into that position. That's like them saying that if we show one traffic accident, we have to show them all. I see traffic accidents on their national news all the time, but I'll bet we don't see all of the accidents.

He was able to get local CBC radio and television in several communities. CBC radio in Whitehorse kept track of us and interviewed me all the way across Canada. But not even they could get any national coverage.

At one time, in Montreal, Quebec, we spotted a CBC television reporter and cameraman just standing on the sidewalk. I rode my hand cycle right past them. Christ pointed at me and told them what I was doing and why. They just said they were busy, waiting for something or someone, and didn't have time. When we came back the same way about fifteen minutes later, they were still waiting and they still ignored us.

Yet at other times, like in Fredricton, New Brunswick, the local CBC stations couldn't do enough for us.

CTV not only gave us regional coverage, but we also made their national broadcast and onto their news network channel for a day. Most of the major newspapers in Canada gave us plenty of press and we even made the front page of a few of them

Right from the beginning we stopped at schools that wanted me to give presentations to their students. We would only be able to talk to the students during the school months so we had to take advantage of every opportunity presented to us.

I tried to use my brace and crutch in every school presentation. I would start talking, sitting on the stage or the floor with my brace beside me. At one point during the presentation I would put the brace on and stand up with my crutch. This would show them how I can become a full participating member of society rather than just a paralyzed guy sitting on a stage.

The concept was simple. This is how Polio survivors in other countries are living. I wanted to show the kids how survivors are interacting with other members of their community.

Now they (the healthy students) are on the ground looking up at a Polio survivor – just like Polio survivors in third world countries are on the ground looking up at healthy people.

I would tell them, "This is what I have to do every day to simply stand up."

It was a good visual for them. Then I would ask them what they learned. I would hold up my crutch and ask them "What is this?" Hold up my brace. Hold up my sandals and ask them what the difference was between the left foot and the right one. One is thicker than the other. Then I would ask "Why do you think that is?"

It's because my right leg is shorter than my left.

At the end of the presentation I would be standing up in my shorts so the children could see me wearing my brace, my shoes and the crutch and I would tell them "This is what I'm able to do because I have these things to help me. Millions of Polio survivors around the world are doing what you're doing right now. What are you doing now?"

"We're sitting on the ground."

"Exactly. And that's how they have to live their lives – sitting on the ground because they don't have these aids."

I didn't do that all the time because places like Rotary meetings, round tables, places where people were eating meals, didn't lend themselves to making that presentation effective. But I used it in every school and the kids were right into it.

Sometimes the kids were able to give something back. The students at the school in Chilliwack, B.C., gave us the money they raised from a pizza lunch.

As we rode into the central regions of British Columbia, the hand cycling itself was a bit of a challenge. There were some pretty substantial hills. One – a place called Six Mile Hill near the town of Savona, B.C., – took me over an hour to get up. The weather wasn't really very good either. Most days were grey, rainy and the clouds just hung really low on the mountains. I could see the snowline up high. Some days it did snow and I think the snow line crept down as fast as I climbed up.

I was wearing long underwear, long sleeved shirts, quilted riding jackets and nylon wind jackets. My legs were protected by wind pants. I had socks, hats, neck warmers, mitts and gloves. I even had hand warmers, those chemical packs you break and they generate heat for four or five hours, inside the mitts. Sometimes that wasn't even enough.

We were close to Lytton, B.C. - it was one of those "Looks like it's a 'Sure sucks to be Ramesh' day!" days. In fact, that was the first place I heard that description from Chris, but it definitely wasn't the last. My fingers were cold as usual but my foot was frozen so we cut the day short. Bertha had just boiled up a pot of water for tea so she and Lynn wrapped the kettle in a towel, then tied it and my feet together in another towel. It felt great and the feeling returned fairly quickly.

I think it was during that extra long rest stop that I suddenly realized that I wasn't the only one working. The road crew was laboring right along with me. I was so caught up in my own efforts I really hadn't taken notice. Chris was constantly on his phone trying to line up more interviews or filing reports to the Whitehorse office. He also edited my daily blog entries.

When he wasn't driving the Suburban, Doug was doing regular maintenance on the vehicles like checking the oil, or filling the water tank in the motor home or emptying the sewage. He would check the GPS and make sure it was working and up to date, then download the data to our website map. He would sit and analyze the map, trying to figure out what we could expect to find down the road.

Bertha and Lynne shared the driving duties in the motor home, but they also did all the housekeeping chores like cooking meals and doing the laundry. And I ate a lot of food, about 5,000 calories per day. A typical breakfast for me would be three eggs, two pieces of toast, a bowl of oatmeal and a banana washed down with milk. I generated a lot of dirty clothes! Bertha was also in charge of telling me not to wipe up messes in the motor home with the tea towel.

She and Lynne also made sure I had a steady supply of oatmeal, bananas, cashews and Gatorade. If people were to judge me by the amount of food I ate on the road, they would probably think I was pregnant. It's astounding how the right food truly is fuel for your body because those things helped me climb the never-ending uphill grades. I drank a lot of Gatorade diluted with water – between nine to twelve liters per day - while I crossed the country. I hated Gatorade before I started the trip and I hate it even more now!

Everyone collected donations. Whenever someone in one vehicle received a donation they would radio the other vehicle and ask them "What have you done for the campaign lately?" Bertha did all the banking and organized financial reports for head office.

The biggest climb I made in the mountains of British Columbia was Messier Summit – 765 meters in one very slow, very grinding climb. That is near a town called Blue River. People use helicopters to go up there for heli-skiing! They were doing that in April, while we were there. I had to make the same ascent by hand and I didn't even get to ski!

I don't think I'm different from most people in liking train whistles. I came to really enjoy them while I was riding up the Fraser Valley because the engineers blew them to show support for Cycle to Walk. Every day I noticed there were more and more honks of support from cars and transport trucks. The trucks were also very respectful and gave us plenty of room when they went past.

When I was a kid we used to think it fun if we held our breath while our parents drove through a tunnel or over a bridge. There were lots of bridges and tunnels in the mountains of British Columbia and, unfortunately, I had to break that rule. It's not that easy to hand cycle while not breathing.

The stretch of highway we couldn't travel was called the Snake Pit. It was on the Fraser Canyon stretch. The Ministry of Transportation strongly suggested we not travel it because it is quite narrow and the road has no shoulders. So we drove for three and a half kilometers and decided we would make up the missed distance at another location. That's when I rode circles around a parking lot to make up for the distance.

I knew we were starting to reach people. As we got close to Kamloops we noticed a red truck backing the wrong way down a highway exit. When it stopped close to us a young man got out with one of those blue Seagram's Crown Royal bags.

"I heard on the radio that you were close to town," he said as he handed Bertha the bag full of coins, "I believe in your cause and I like what you're doing."

What a good feeling to hear that after all the cold, snow and rain of the past few days.

I also learned something very weird about my journey. Not only were people stopping by the side of the road to talk to us or donate but other species were interested as well. Cows stopped grazing as I went by. Horses would trot along the fence line with me or gallop across a field to look at me. I guess, when all you have to do all day is eat grass, drink water and sleep day after day after day, anything different that might happen to break the boredom is a welcome distraction.

I liked to think they knew we were on the road for a good cause. Still, you'd think they'd never seen a guy on a hand cycle before. I wondered if I might find myself as easily distracted because my days were going to be full of eating, drinking and pedaling, day after day. It made it easy to relate intellectually to the cow.

Sitting down low on the bike also gave me an interesting perspective on the mountain goats we saw and the cows who always seemed to be so far above me. Quite often I would look up and think to myself, "There is a cow in the sky."

When riding a hand cycle a long way every day, I had too much time to think about stuff and see things, like cows, completely out of context.

There was a lot of British Columbia to go through. Not only were we heading west to east, but we were also angling north so we would hook up with the Yellowhead Highway that would take us into Alberta.

Near Clearwater, B.C., a woman named Joan stopped her car to tell me her neighbor had Polio and what we were doing touched her heart. A gentleman named Mr. Carefoot waited by the side of the road for me and we talked about our experiences. He had been affected by Polio in 1953 and was paralyzed for a while from his neck down. Now he could walk and use his arms and hands. He gave us a donation and went back to his car.

A group of people stood on the road cheering for us. One of them had seen us back in the Fraser Canyon, just outside of Vancouver, told her friends and here they were to show their support.

In Valemount, B.C., I had an opportunity to go for a ride with Jean Ann McKirdy – a member of Canada's Cycling Team. And I found out why people move to small towns in central B.C. We met a lady from Africa who had thrown a dart at a map of Canada to determine where she was going to move. The dart landed in Tete Jaune Cache just down the road from Valemount. So here she was, running a coffee shop. She also told me she had witnessed "crawlers" in Africa and applauded the message of Cycle to Walk.

During one of my school presentations there were a number of parents in attendance. I talked about the fact that eleven per cent of children in Canada hadn't been vaccinated against Polio.

Parents aren't obliged to vaccinate their children. Immunizations are strongly recommended, but parents do have the right to decline. Some education acts state that children must be vaccinated to be allowed to attend school but if the parent has an objection, such as religion, the children are permitted to go to school if the parent signs a form identifying why they weren't vaccinated.

"In Canada," I said, "people are becoming complacent toward vaccinating themselves and their children against Polio because they think Polio is a non-issue. The reality is that as long as there's a single case of Polio in our world, no country is Polio-free."

As I was saying good-bye to one of the families the mother – who has a daughter about 12 years old – was crying.

"I think I need to tell you," she explained to me, "Because I think you need to know. I haven't been vaccinated. None of my children have been vaccinated. But your visit here has made me realize I need to get that done. And I will."

Kamloops was our first long break since leaving Victoria. An opportunity to rest up, restock supplies, visit some schools, go to Rotary meetings and media interviews. We got an email from a woman named Jacquie Lowndes, asking if we could make a trip to Salmon Arm, B.C., to visit her father. We weren't sure if we should make the trip because Salmon Arm was a considerable way off our route.

But Jacquie persisted. In another email she said "If something happens that it is not going to be convenient, I will take Dad to Kamloops or anywhere else on the planet to make it happen." Then she added, "Dad's name is John Sayer."

I still wasn't fully aware of John's role in my adoption, but I did know he had been involved in my life at the orphanage and had visited us once in Whitehorse a long time ago. My parents told me "You must meet this man." Doug was concerned because our budget was tight but we, as a team, decided that Doug and I should make the trip.

Chris had us heavily booked with media in Kamloops, but there was one day that he had left empty as a rest day, so Doug and I drove to Salmon Arm. When we got to the seniors home where John was living the staff met us at the door and told us that Jacquie was just bringing her dad down.

When he arrived, Jacquie introduced me to him, but at first he really didn't understand who I was. I could see it meant a lot to his family that we were there. As Jacquie, his wife Anneke and his other daughter Judy Holman explained to him I was the little boy he had taken to the doctor's office in Coimbatore, I could see his face light up. There were tears in his eyes.

I didn't realize he took me to the doctor's appointments. That was something I learned in Salmon Arm. This was also the first time I heard the pen story and how it related to the decision made by Lloyd Axworthy.

John visited us in Whitehorse in the 1980s and had some pictures of that visit. One of the images in our logo for Cycle to Walk was based upon a photo supplied by my parents - which he had taken. So I had met him since I had arrived in Canada, but made no connection because I was too young.

In the end it meant so much to him that we made the trip to meet him. He kept wanting to touch me like he was trying to figure out if I was real or not. With what I learned about him that day - even if he hadn't reacted the way he did - I still would have been fine with meeting him. To see the emotion in his daughters. His wife. In him. I could tell our effort meant so much to the family. John had talked to them a lot about his experience in India.

For me, it was overwhelming to know this man had such an enormous influence in my being given the opportunities I've had. When we left, Jacquie handed me a note.

"Thank you for taking the time to meet with Dad. God speed."

John Sayer died while we were still on the road. I got a package from Jacquie in January (2009). It had a Christmas card. A copy of his obituary... And a pen.

As each 1000 kilometers was reached the distance was marked by the road crew. This stake, marking 2000 kilometers, was planted by (L to R) Carly Ray, Bertha Ayers, Chris Madden, me and Doug Ayers.

D…as in dumbbell

✦

We were cycling through Jasper National Park and there were mountain sheep on the road ahead of us. With big horns. We were going pretty slow. It is comfortable to see wild sheep from a car, but it's much more intimidating to meet them on a hand cycle. The sheep were taller than me.

Lynne got out of the motorhome and started walking alongside me as we were going through this herd of sheep and she says to the sheep, "Now. Now. It's Okay. It's Okay."

To the sheep!

I just looked at her. I said nothing because she was doing such a good job of calming the sheep who really didn't care whether I was there or not. But I was thinking "Lynne! They're the ones with the horns! They're wild animals. They could charge me. I'm the one you should be reassuring!"

We encountered deer on the side of the road a few times. They'd see me and jump a bit. Then stop and stare. Then jump some more. And stop and stare. When they realized there was nothing to fear, they would just stand there and watch me. Once I had to stop cycling to let three elk cross the road in front of me. A couple of moose. And I saw two donkeys. They weren't crossing the road but it is worth mentioning.

I saw bear tracks on the shoulder of the road and quite often felt like animal bait. We did have a bear attack strategy worked out. This was the "risk management" plan I mentioned to my sister Jenny in Victoria.

If a bear came out of the bush after me, Chris was supposed to jump out of the truck and use my crutch as a club to hit the bear. I didn't have a lot of confidence in that plan and neither did Chris. Whatever plan we came up with, I think our reaction would have been a lot different than what we actually had planned. I don't know how it might have turned out but I'm not convinced Chris would actually have gotten out of the truck.

But there was no need for concern. Other than a lynx that crossed the road in front of me in northern Ontario, and one fox, we never did encounter or even see any wild animal that would have wanted to do more than nibble on my ears.

Most problems were dogs. They would charge out and actually run in front of the tires or block the way. I was nervous several times that I might get bitten or get bowled right over by them. Some of them weighed as much as I did, they had the ability to get out of the way and I didn't. If it hadn't been for Chris's voice I probably would have collided with a few of them. When he yelled at them out of the window of the truck, you could see them flinch away.

The best encounter I had with wildlife was a bug flying into my helmet. It told me that spring had finally arrived and it was getting warm.

The warm weather turned all the frozen dirt on the shoulders of the Yellowhead into muck. It flew up off the tires. Came at me from the spray from passing vehicles. My face, head, back, chest, arms, legs and toes were coated. Add to that all of the chain grease that sprayed back at me from the bike chain and accumulated on my jersey every day as I cycled. You can imagine I was pretty gross.

One particularly filthy day I was cycling down the Yellowhead, and a thought popped into my head – there's that 'too much time to think during a long cycling day' thing again. It's important to remember that all that dirt comes off, but elsewhere in the world, there's a culture of "crawlers." Children. Teenagers. Adults. Who had their legs paralyzed for life because they didn't get the vaccine.

In the lives of "crawlers" they are almost always dirty. They don't have the luxury of crawling into a bathtub at the end of the day or standing under a shower. It's donations and awareness that will get them out of the dirt. It's donations and awareness that will provide those few small drops of vaccine that can ensure that their children, our children will never have to crawl.

One reporter who interviewed me just after we crossed the B.C./Alberta border asked if he could take a measurement of my bicep. I agreed, as long as he also measured my right calf. That condition showed this wasn't about cycling across the country to see how big my muscles got. It was about bringing attention to Canada and the rest of the world that Polio continues to paralyze and kill children needlessly.

ALBERTA

April 30- May 20, 2008

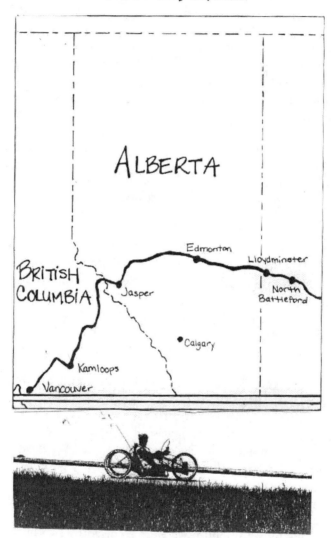

My right bicep muscle is 16.5 inches around, which is fairly large. The important fact is that my calf is only 7.5 inches around, which is about half of what it should be for a male of my age in good shape.

After our stop in Edson, Alberta, there were some letters published in the 'Edson Leader' from kids I had talked to while we were there. I was pretty excited to find they had taken the Cycle to Walk message seriously enough to put it in writing.

"My name is Lauren and yesterday something marvelous changed my life! I am home-schooled and my father is in Rotary. He was going to a speech so he wanted mother to come. At Rotary, there was someone there named Ramesh Ferris (pronounced Raw-mesh). He needed a place to stay so mother said he could stay at our house, of course...I think it is so amazing because he had a disability and is changing the world. Terry Fox had gone half way around Canada. Ramesh has gone one-seventh. Ramesh says to follow your dreams.

Lauren
Grade 3"

"Ramesh (Raw-mesh) is awesome. He's like Terry Fox on wheels. He's really cool. So are his helpers. On May 5 he marked 1,000 kilometers and on a hand sicle!!!

Samuel
Grade 5"

I love talking with children. They see the importance of what needs to be done to eradicate Polio. They get so excited about it and want to learn more.

When we reached each thousand kilometers we would write 'Cycle to Walk' on a survey stake, the date and the distance – one thousand, two thousand or whichever – take photos, then stick it in the ground if we could.

There were bigger rides into bigger cities later in the trip, but the ride into Edmonton, Alberta, was the first major event in my mind and the one that had the most symbolic meaning for me.

It wasn't just riding into a city. It was riding into the city where I arrived in Canada in 1982 and met my Dad for the first time. When we arrived at the 'Welcome to Edmonton" sign, who was there but a photographer from the Edmonton Journal which was the first newspaper to run an article about my adoption in 1982. It was nice to be able to say "I'm back" and "this is what we're doing." It meant a lot to me

As we rode into Edmonton we were escorted by two huge concrete pumper trucks provided by A&B Concrete Pumping. They guided us to the parking lot of All Weather Windows where we were greeted by about 60 employees who took time off work to be there for us.

There were speeches, photos and cheques from the Daytona Group of Companies, which owns both A&B and All Weather, presented to Cycle to Walk. It was a great welcome to Edmonton for Cycle to Walk, but it wasn't Chris's best day.

As I was riding along behind the pumper trucks, Chris was talking on his phone to the executives of All Weather Windows, trying to get the proper spellings and pronunciations so when I stood up to say thank you, I would have all the information in front of me.

They were spelling out the name of the company president, Gord Weibe, but Chris was having trouble hearing them over the road noise.

"Could you repeat that?" he asked.

"Weibe. W...E...I...B...E," said the voice on the telephone.

"Weibe. That's W...E...I...and, is that B - as in bumblebee or D - as in dumbbell?" Doug just about drove off the road at that point. There was silence on the phone.

"Oops," said Chris, "I think that was a poor choice of words."

"We were just thinking the same thing," said the phone

I don't recall whether they teased him about it or not when we arrived in Edmonton, but we never let him forget. He didn't make that mistake again and I doubt he ever will but we told that story to everyone we could, all the way to Cape Spear.

I spoke to rehabilitation recipients at the University of Alberta's Steadward Centre for Personal and Physical Achievement. They were an amazing group of people.

I don't know where I would be today if I didn't have a positive attitude. I told them about going to Easter Seal Camps in Squamish, B.C., when I was younger and talking with other people who had limited mobility. Some felt sorry for themselves and didn't focus on their abilities. I always try to demonstrate to people the things I can do, rather than focus on what I can't.

Going through rehabilitation myself, I know it's an extreme test on one's patience, body and ego. There were times when it made me cry and I thought I just wanted to give up. In reality I knew that's not what I wanted. So I had just kept pushing forward. You can and will achieve all you set out to do.

I was given the privilege of talking to an international group of students at Grant McEwan College in Edmonton one afternoon. There were about 60 students in the English as a Second Language program. It was a challenge to know whether or not they understood my words. But they definitely understood the message. I was touched by the kind words of encouragement, in every language they spoke. One of them, a doctor from Afghanistan, told me that the work of Cycle to Walk is both essential and appreciated.

Rick Hansen, the Man in Motion and CEO of the Rick Hansen
Foundation, wished me "good luck"" prior to starting Cycle to Walk

Doug and Bertha Ayers. I couldn't have had better road parents.
They continually taught me lessons in humanity.

My godmother Lynne Morris and communications guru Chris Madden.

Allon Reddoch and I enjoy some time together.

The first handcycle I ever saw and rode. The man riding this cycle in Coimbatore, India, designed and built it himself.

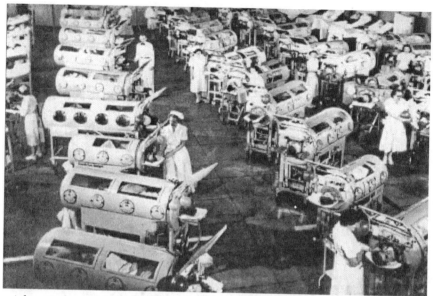

A hospital ward full of Iron Lungs keeping Polio victims alive in the 1950s.

*John Sayer and I were brought together one last time in
Salmon Arm, B.C., by his daughter Jacquie Lowndes.*

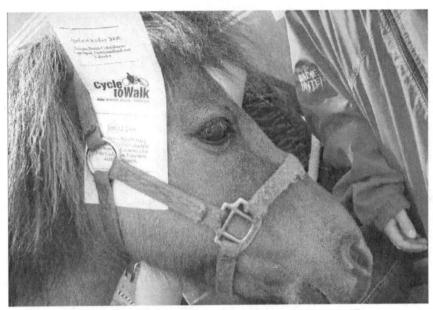

Even the animals got into the spirit of Cycle to Walk.

Inside the motorhome, our base for the entire six months.
(L to R) me, Carly Ray, Doug and Bertha.

I didn't feel that Terry Fox's monument near Thunder Bay, Ontario, was a place for me to talk about my cause. It was a chance to honor one of my role models and share his space for a short time.

Breaking the tape at the start of Cycle to Walk in Victoria, B.C., on April 12, 2008.

*David Onley, the Lieutenant Governor of Ontario,
showed me his electric scooter and talked about what it did
for him while I explained what Little Brace did for me.*

*Former Canadian Immigration Minister Lloyd Axworthy played
such a significant role in my life that I felt I had to meet him
and say "thank you" almost 30 years after my adoption.*

The board room at Sanofi-Pasteur in Toronto, Ontario. (L to R) Sanofi CEO and president Luis Barreto, unknown, Doug Ayers, Polio historian Chris Rutty – who I consulted in preparing for Cycle to Walk.

I hope we reminded the Prime Minister that Polio is still a threat. (L to R) Me, Allon Reddoch, Prime Minister Stephen Harper, Bertha Ayers.

At Potato World in Florenceville, New Brunwick. (L to R) Marilyn Strong, a director of the Harrison McCain Foundation, Chris Madden, unknown, Allison McCain, chairman of McCain Foods Limited.

My Dad and I were ready for the final ride to the Atlantic Ocean at Cape Spear on October 1, 2008, and my mother carried Little Brace.

Talking with fishermen at Petty Harbour, Newfoundland.

Kip Veale, Doug and Bertha in Halifax, Nova Scotia.

*South Korea's Dong Kurn Lee, president of Rotary International in
2008-2009, me and Dr. Bob Scott, Chair of Rotary International's
Polio Plus Committee during my trip to India in November, 2008.*

*Meeting up with another cross country fund raising
journey, Matt Hill and The Run for One Planet*

Another of the students there told me she knew someone who actually contracted Polio from the vaccine. That can happen. It's one in a million. Doesn't seem like much, unless you are the one in a million.

I told her that, while we can't make that one feel any less traumatized by the event, we also had to take into account the millions who didn't get Polio because of the vaccine.

We were in Edmonton for Mother's Day. Mothers make big decisions in the lives of children. My biological mother made a pretty significant decision for me. My Canadian mother made the decision that I should be as independent as possible and, most of all, she believed in my ability to do anything.

Mothers need to make the decision to get their children immunized to protect them from Polio. I know my mother in India would have made that decision if she had access to the vaccination.

As we continued east from Edmonton, one thing became very clear.

Whomever told us that the prevailing winds on the prairies went from west to east – was wrong.

The trip to the world's largest Pysanka (Ukrainian Easter Egg), in Vegreville, Alberta, was done in a crosswind that easily reached 30 to 40 kilometers per hour. The wind was so strong in some areas that when I got off the bike for breaks, it tipped over on its side. When it wasn't blowing across me, it was blowing directly at me. Now I truly have an understanding of why it's much faster to fly west across Canada than east. But the perogies and cabbage rolls and other traditional Ukrainian dishes the Vegreville Rotary Club treated us to when we arrived made it all worth while.

The next night we went out for dinner in Vermillion, Alberta, and our server, seeing our jackets and T-shirts, asked us what we were up to. When I explained to her that I was a Polio survivor from India she gave me a strange look, "Polio? You don't look like you're a hundred and ten years old." We explained Cycle to Walk to her and explained that it is still a health threat in the world. Many Canadians share her sentiments and think Polio is a worry of the past.

That server exemplifies what Cycle to Walk was all about. We need to raise awareness and funds to end a disease that many think has already been beaten.

As we approached Lloydminister and the Saskatchewan/Alberta border, we had a change of road crew. Lynne, who would go ahead on the road and throw the ripped up bits of tires from the transport trucks into the ditch so I wouldn't have to ride over or around them, was heading back to Whitehorse.

A close friend of mine from my days at the Anglican Church Diocese of Algoma's Youth Synod at Camp Manitou, Carly Ray, came from Nipigon, Ontario, to join us. We went to the camp together for three or four years. It's an annual summer camp held on the August long weekend that brings together kids from all over northern Ontario. We lost touch for years until Cycle to Walk brought us back together.

Carly didn't really pick up the rubber bits for me but she was a better singer than Lynne and kept Bertha entertained during those long days on the road. She also seemed to be able to anticipate my needs and would often have things like 'Little Brace' or my crutch ready for me before I even thought of asking for them. She made sure my riding clothes were ready for me every day. Which was good because it gave Bertha a break from having to read my mind.

I learned some prairie wisdom in Saskatchewan. When cows huddle together in the middle of fields to protect themselves against the weather, it's not a good sign for cyclists.

I also discovered what those beautiful pictures of the Canadian prairies on the tourism posters don't tell you. They show you the blue skies, the puffy clouds, the miles of wheat and the sunshine – and those things are there. What they seem to leave out are the headwinds or the gravel sections with construction signs telling motorists to "Save your windshield. Slow down." Another myth busted was the one about the prairies being flat. They look flat at first glance, but every time you reach a stream or river, there seems to be a long downhill to reach the bridge and an even longer, steeper uphill on the other side.

I had no idea that grain elevators and telecommunication towers were so large. We could identify where the next community was by spotting one or the other. They would look close but we knew they could actually still be a couple of hours away. I'll be honest. It was very discouraging at times. All I could do was be patient and know that, eventually, I would make it to the next town.

For the longest time I never believed I needed sunscreen because of my dark skin. But now I had this odd pattern on top of my head. Even when I wasn't wearing my bike helmet, it looked like I was. Where the helmet blocked the sun, the skin was a lighter color. Where it didn't cover my head, the skin was much darker. It even got sun burnt. I learned the hard way that, regardless of skin color, it's definitely important to ensure protection from harsh ultraviolet rays.

However, it was nice to learn that chocolate people such as myself can get a tan. It was a more natural way to get my teeth whiter without brushing.

We met great people alongside the road. In one construction site a worker ran across the road to give a donation to Carly then, as I cycled by, shouted, "Good luck man. I know you can do it." During one break, three power line technicians from Sask Power walked over to visit and share stories about how Polio had affected each of their families.

In Kenaston, Saskatchewan, we got donations from the town council, then a personal donation from the mayor. The owner of the hotel gave us dinner and we encountered a man who apparently was the town drunk. He made me somewhat uncomfortable but Doug and Bertha are kind to everyone they meet and we stopped to listen to him.

He had a lot to say about nothing, but when he found out what Cycle to Walk was all about, he reached into his pocket and donated a very crumpled, very smelly five dollar bill. He had Polio as a child and he was affected – but not as badly as his aunt who has one leg shorter than the other.

I should have put him in perspective and not based my initial response on a conditioned reflex imposed on me by society – one that is also often imposed by other's reactions to me. Next time I'll work harder to not base my judgment on first impressions but, like Doug and Bertha, always give someone the benefit of my doubt.

They were truly the best choice for on-road parents I could have had. All the way across the country they kept teaching me lessons in humanity.

I got my one and only injury of the trip at Ron and Dean Studney's (Jody's parents) house in North Battleford. I slipped on a throw rug that slid unexpectedly on a hardwood floor and sprained my ankle. Fortunately, it didn't stop me from cycling. I got a nice red and blue soft cast put on at Union Hospital and I had to walk slowly – but I could still walk. I don't think people realize how important that is to me. Everyone takes it for granted. But for me, it was and still is, a gift.

It didn't matter what time of day or night it is, I was always encouraged when I was reminded of the importance of our message.

When I was growing up, my mom would enforce a strict ten in the morning to ten at night rule. All outgoing and incoming phone calls had to be made within those hours – no exceptions unless it was a matter of life or death and even then we had to be really, really sure. People from other time zones can't always be sure of what time it is where they're calling – so they call any time.

My cell phone rang around three in the morning and I answered it without even looking to see who was calling. It turned out to be a man called Lalantha. We've never met, but he found out about Cycle to Walk on Facebook and was calling me from Australia just to wish me luck. He is originally from India and told me that Cycle to Walk should involve other countries in the future. There are good reasons for more exceptions to my mother's phone rule.

The message, I believe, did reach into other countries and beyond the scope of where we could be and what we could do. I looked at the Rotary International news website one night. There was an article about my trip on line and at the end there were comments from people in Utah, India, Nepal and parts of Canada we had no opportunity to reach.

I would like to take Cycle to Walk to another country. At one of the Rotary luncheons I met an American from California who got quite excited about Cycle to Walk. When he got back home, he told me, he was going to look into the possibility of me doing the same journey across the United States.

There seem to be a lot of hand cyclists in Saskatchewan. In Saskatoon I rode into the city with three other Polio survivors: Donna Spratt, Dale Schiissler and Ronald Johnson. All of them had contracted Polio in 1955 – just before the Salk tests were conducted.

When we reached Regina, Saskatchewan, three more hand cyclists joined me behind the Regina City Police escort who took us through the city to the Saskatchewan Legislative Building.

The "Joy of Effort" is one of the main motivational themes for students at Jack Mackenzie Elementary School in Regina. It's a motto that fit very well with Cycle to Walk. I felt joy when I talked to the students about Polio eradication, education and rehabilitation. Knowing that together we can help Polio survivors live with dignity. Those kids were excited about living their motivational theme.

When I was washing my hands one morning in Portage La Prairie, Manitoba, I noticed the bar of soap had a plastic wrapping which read "Thank you for being here." That made me feel so appreciated and it was a reminder to me of the great things this campaign could accomplish. Sometimes you don't have to look too far. The message may be in the soap.

Winnipeg, Manitoba, was going to be big for us. This was Chris's home town and he must have called in every favor he was owed and probably a few he now owes. He rounded up all of his friends and told them to bring along some of their friends. He called them a "Rent a crowd for Ramesh."

The police led us into town along with some cyclists and a couple of people on roller blades. I was able to talk to a good sized crowd at The Forks. Then we went to the Manitoba Children' Museum where we were able to put on a unique presentation which included me demonstrating the hand cycle and talking about Polio. Chris did some ball juggling and made balloon animals for the kids. I attempted to make a balloon animal, but only ended up making sausage links.

SASKATCHEWAN

May 20 - June 5, 2008

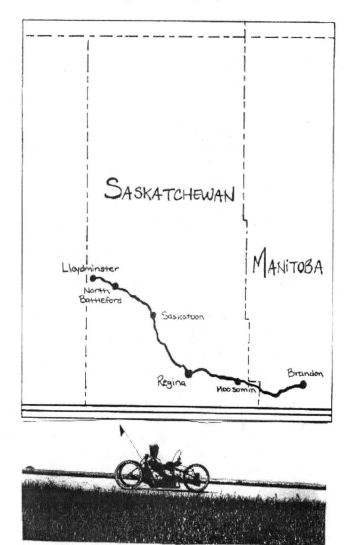

After I spoke at St. Bartholemew Anglican Church the next morning Carly and I went to visit the Winnipeg Hindu Temple. When entering a temple, it's respectful to take one's shoes off, but I can't walk without my shoes. Members of the temple helped us brainstorm to find a solution. We decided to use plastic shopping bags over my shoes so I could walk into the temple and discuss Cycle to Walk with members of Winnipeg's Indo-Canadian community.

Doug and Bertha's son Jaime and his wife Charlene joined them for the day. Chris was able to spend some time with his parents. It was nice that some of the team members could be fathers or with their father on Father's Day. I thought about my dad quite a bit that day. He has been so much of a role model for me, with all the love, friendship, support and guidance he gave me over all my life.

One of the things he said to me which I'll always reuse is "Allow me to take the risk of failure in hopes to succeed." I love him very much.

One of the most moving meetings we went to was a barbeque hosted by the Post-Polio Network of Manitoba. Both Bertha and I almost cried when we arrived. There were an amazing number of people on chairs, in wheelchairs and some with oxygen tanks. I was truly honored to meet them and hear so many personal stories about how Polio had touched them.

Our reality today is so different from that of the past when these people lived in fear of Polio every time someone got a flu-like infection in their home or neighborhood. They talked of watching their friends or families walking around one day and sick or dead the next. Of people travelling on airplanes and getting the flu, only to find it was Polio and they would never use their legs again. It sickens me to think that people in the world continue to live in fear. It's not acceptable. Polio shouldn't exist.

At the barbeque Art Braid gave me some tremendous words of encouragement. He recalled his days working as the Manitoba provincial chair for Rick Hansen's Man In Motion campaign and he could see I had the same drive and determination as Rick. It was a great honor to be compared to one of my role models – particularly by someone who worked so closely with him.

It was at times like this that we knew we were protected and helped in miraculous ways and sometimes we met people, like the people at the barbeque, who were gifts from God. Doug and Bertha called the people who encouraged us, provided us with accommodations or who volunteered all along the way, "The Angels in our Path." They were put there to add understanding and new dimension to our own Polio awareness. The same way we were put in theirs to bring hope and awareness that others are there to work to eradicate this disease forever.

I felt like a salesman the next night but that was part of the whole mission. We were there to sell Polio eradication. We were invited to sell T-shirts and spread the message at a Winnipeg Goldeyes baseball game at Canwest Park. The people were there to watch baseball, not talk Polio. Most just walked right by and some people would just stare at us. Others did come up and talk. Most of those bought T-shirts and gave donations.

When I suggested to three teenagers that they would look great in a new Cycle to Walk T-shirt, they just scowled at me like I was some crazy man. Still I didn't give up. I informed a man who was walking by that his shoelaces were undone. He stopped and started to tie his shoes. I took the liberty of handing him a brochure and asked if he wanted to buy a T-shirt. He bought one, then finished tying up his shoelace.

I finally met Lloyd Axworthy face-to-face for the first time in both of our lives in Winnipeg. Here was a man who changed a decision and allowed me into the country. He was the president of the University of Manitoba and we met in his office.

I showed him 'Little Brace.' I gave him a photocopy of the article with his name in it and an autographed picture of me on which I wrote, "Your decision allowed me to walk. Thank you." I thought it important to share that with him. He was taken aback by it. I believe it really meant a lot to him that we took the time to meet him and say that to him.

I don't think politicians get enough credit for the positive decisions they make. We just focus so much on the negative – which we need to do as well because, every decision they make affects peoples lives. When good stories happen, society doesn't focus on them. We're more intrigued by the number of bodies lying on the ground than by the number of lives being saved.

*My favorite part of the entire six months was time spent with
children telling my story, showing what Polio can do and
creating awareness that they can play a role in eradicating it*

We Need to be Really Bothered

✦

People have always been doing something like running or biking across Canada or the United States to attract attention to good causes. Terry Fox was probably one of the first who did it despite having only one good leg. It was the fact that he displayed such courage and strength in the face of his limited mobility that caught the imagination of Canada, then the world.

It didn't hurt his cause that cancer in his time and in the years that followed his death was the Polio of a new generation. Rick Hansen's Man in Motion was the same kind of trip. It was unique and different and people were still caught up in the excitement of Terry.

It's harder to stand out today. There must be forty or fifty different cross-country fund raising campaigns going on in Canada every summer. We came across several other programs that used the word "Cycle" or "Walk" in their three word title. Sometimes those similarities worked for us and other times it didn't.

At the Goldeyes game in Winnipeg a man came up to our table looking for information on "Cycle to Work." The name didn't mean anything to us, but we found out it was a local environmental initiative to encourage people to ride their bikes to work rather than driving a car. It didn't take us long to straighten out the difference. It turned out he was a reporter for the Winnipeg Free Press. He made a few phone calls and lined up an interview for us the next morning. It's amazing how things work out!

Then there was "Wheel to Walk." This was Les McLaughlin, Harvey Uppal, Charlie Cetinski and Chuck Mealing, who handcycled across the country to raise awareness and funds for chronic spinal cord injury.

MANITOBA

June 6 -19, 2008

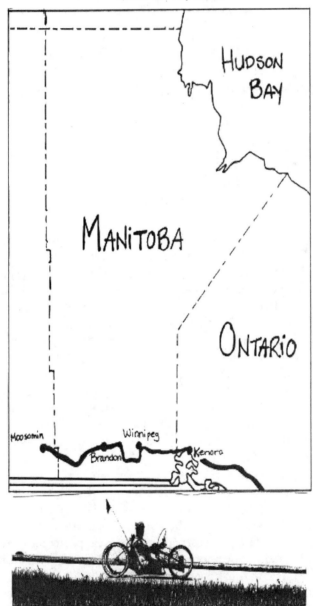

We stayed at the same hotel as they did in Meaford, Ontario, which caused a little confusion at the front desk where the poor clerk tried to sort out who was staying where and who was looking for whom. We had an opportunity to share our dreams, challenges and road stories before they took off ahead of us. They moved a lot faster than us and finished at Cape Spear about six weeks before we did.

We did have one more incident that involved them although they were a long way ahead of us by then. Just outside of Fredericton, New Brunswick, a couple stopped on the side of the road and walked back to the motor home. Doug and Bertha were outside talking to them and I stood in the door. It turned out they were looking for Wheel to Walk and we told them our last report already had them across Nova Scotia.

I started to explain to them what Cycle to Walk was about, but the man just looked at me and said, "Yeh. But they're paralyzed and all you've got is some leg problems."

I've always thought of part of my life as snippets of television comedy episodes. People have said the weirdest things to me. Like I've been judged by my appearance my whole life and people have made assumptions about me because they haven't taken the time to understand.

That particular episode I wasn't wearing shorts so it wasn't apparent that people could see the effects of what Polio had done to me. I just thought, "Who are you to judge me!?" I felt offended. I felt I had taken the time to explain what Cycle to Walk was, what we were doing, then to hear that. I thought "Well. I'm done with this person."

When I got back to Whitehorse I was going through a bunch of mail. One of the letters was from that couple. They thanked me for sharing my story and then told me that Polio had affected her family when she was young and wished me well in spreading the message. That's one of those 'God works in mysterious ways' things that we are always hearing about in church.

There were a few episodes like that where people are trying to be funny, but unintentionally inflict pain. In Valemount, B.C., Doug and I were in a small gift shop and this gentleman, probably in his 60s, looked at me, at my legs and said "Looks like you've got a flat tire there." I was insulted but I thought "Keep a positive attitude." I smiled at him and moved on.

In Edson, Alberta, we were walking into a hotel and there were about 15 people in ball caps and work boots standing in the lobby. They're all talking and, as soon as I walk in, they all just stopped and stared at us.

It reminded me of when my friend and I had decided to go to the IMAX theatre in Victoria before the official start of Cycle to Walk. Both of us are Polio survivors. We're both using crutches. We're about the same height. And we're both chocolate. This older lady walked towards us and, as she got close, she piped up, "Looks like you two boys have seen better days."

I just laugh in disbelief most times. I just deposit it. It's not me, it's them. It's my attitude that's gotten me this far without actually killing someone.

There are so many ways to cross Canada for a purpose.

Martha Birkett rode a horse to raise money and awareness for the Children's Wish Foundation – which is all about fulfilling the dreams of terminally ill children. She rode from Ottawa, Ontario, back to her home in Cochrane, Alberta, then to Bearspaw (just west of Calgary) where she finished her 'Giddy Up for Wishes' campaign in early July. We met her near Moosomin in Saskatchewan.

We ran into Jim Razeau a couple of times on his cross-Canada cycle to raise funds for Sick Children's Hospital. The first time he zoomed past me near Wawa in northern Ontario. The next time was in Meaford, Ontario. He had finished his trip and just wanted to ride with me again and support Cycle to Walk.

In Saskatoon, two women cycling from Kamloops, B.C., to Regina, Saskatchewan under the banner of 'Right to Play' – an organization whose purpose is to raise awareness and interest in availing children in Third World countries access to sports – rode with me. We had earlier seen them in Kamloops.

The 'Run for One Planet' is a pretty ambitious adventure. We encountered them near Marathon, Ontario. Matt Hill and Stephanie Tait were running a marathon (42.2 kilometers) every day, but they were not just crossing Canada. They were spending a carbon neutral year running around the North American continent to raise money for and inspire environmental action. We ended up on the ferry from Nova Scotia to Newfoundland with them three months later.

Just outside of Marathon we came across three people who were taking part in the 'Multifaith Walk Against Violence'. One of them was a Calgary Imam, Syed Soharwardy – the founder of the Islamic Supreme Council of Canada and Muslims Against Terrorism. The walk had started April 20 in Halifax, Nova Scotia, and they were walking to Victoria. Soharwardy planned to walk the entire distance while others would join them for shorter periods.

What was even more amazing was the fact that we had heard of all of these journeys and they had heard of us before we ever met. There's even an organization called the Creative Crossing Society of Canada.

Safety was essential for not only myself, but for the road team, other motorists and community members. That was further impressed upon us when Daniel Hurtubise and Daniel Carriere were killed by a vehicle that struck them from behind on June 29. They were riding their bicycles across Canada for the Juvenile Diabetes Research Foundation.

It was a very sad day when we learned of their deaths. We hadn't met them but there is a personal connection between all the people who cross Canada for a deserving cause.

There were a few times when we were told by provincial authorities not to travel on the Trans Canada Highway, but to use secondary roads for safety reasons. Nova Scotia actually initially imposed restrictions on us crossing bridges or passing through towns that would have made it virtually impossible for us to ride through the province – but they relaxed those requirements when we were just hours away from landing in the province.

Terry Fox had been told by the police to get off the main highway in Quebec and run on secondary roads. People also intentionally forced him off the road occasionally.

There were a few incidents where people, impatient about having to wait behind the escort vehicle and facing on-coming traffic, actually passed us on the right hand side of the road – endangering not only themselves but also the very vulnerable Ramesh Ferris on his hand cycle. Or they passed with the intention of cutting right back into their lane in front of the escort vehicle, only to realize at the last minute that there was something in front of the vehicle – me. Apparently they couldn't or didn't read the sign on the back of the trailer that cautioned there was a "Cyclist Ahead" or acknowledged the flashing yellow warning light.

A lot of the people crossing the country were upset they weren't getting more publicity. When we started out with Cycle to Walk we felt that it wouldn't be an effective way of raising money or media interest unless we could educate people about Polio. There's a lot of accountability and pressure when you represent a charity and…unless you can put some meaning behind what you're doing…unless you can get that message out…journeys like mine aren't worth doing.

Allon – who was really the driving force behind Cycle to Walk – and I believe that our campaign worked really well. It disturbed people like it was supposed to.

This journey took longer than some – one fund raiser took five days to cross the country. That was the fastest one we came across. The majority took between two and four months. We took six months.

We were better organized than most. There was a huge amount of volunteer hours going on behind the scenes. "Route champions" phoning from Whitehorse to find billets at the other end of the country. Organizing church meetings, Rotary luncheons and dinners. The schools. There was a lot of time and effort put specifically into developing the message and preparing me to deliver it. I think that's what actually was missing from most of the other campaigns.

The message actually operated on several levels and it was up to Chris to make them all work together. Meetings, events and talks had mostly been set up by the board members, community volunteers, route champions and office staff in Whitehorse. They did the best they could based upon our planned agenda and their perception of what was happening on the road, but it took Chris to fine tune them into the reality of what was actually going on. It set us apart because we made a conscious effort to have the media involved in the educational aspect.

There was the hand cycle itself. It was different and interesting. Everyone wanted a picture of it in action. A lot of kids and parents took rides on it. Almost all the reporters wanted to talk about it and I often had to really work to get the interviews back on track with our message. We had over 200 interviews and photo opportunities across the country. That was good for families and parents who didn't have the chance to see us, or meet us and who didn't know anything about Polio.

On the community level we went to Rotary meetings and church services. More might have been possible. We found that people really didn't care whether I had climbed an 18 degree hill or rode 160 kilometers in one day. They were there to hear my message. For a lot of those groups it was "preaching to the converted", but even the converted need to be reminded occasionally of why they converted in the first place.

There was a very concerted effort to get endorsements from political leaders because realistically – while individual donations are wonderful - the amount of money required to accomplish the goal of Polio eradication needs organizations like Rotary International, the Bill and Melinda Gates Foundation and especially governments. All it would take for the eradication initiative to disappear is for Canada or a few other countries to say they have a better use for the money elsewhere.

What the Cycle to Walk Society did was approach government at many levels – government ministers, mayors, Provincial premiers, the Prime Minister, city councilors, lieutenant governors, members of parliament and encourage them to publicly support the campaign and the eradication initiative. That worked really well. We met a lot of them, again with as much media attention as we could get, and most gave us letters of endorsement.

It gave us reassurance that the funding would be available for the initiative and that's one aspect of the campaign that most people didn't think about.

Then there was the part I loved the most – being in the schools and talking to the kids. They were attentive. They didn't know anything about my disease, but they asked good questions and were thinking about it.

There were times when I was frustrated with the publicity. When I was tired and Chris and Doug and Bertha were tired. It just seemed that things weren't coming together just right. I would go stomping around – as best I can stomp – thinking "If you're not going to do it, I'll do it myself. It doesn't matter how tired I am. If you're too tired, then I'll do it. I'll get up early and phone the media or set up an event."

A classic line the office staff often used was "Ramesh. You focus on cycling and let go. We'll handle everything up here in the office." I just had to calm myself down and appreciate the skills they had and the time they were committing.

When Terry Fox was trying to raise public awareness of his run, he would get on the phone and try to set up an event or wake up the media. That was me before everyone got involved. I had to do the solo pitch to get people to buy into my goal. It was hard to let go of that, even when we were actually on the road.

In the end it all seemed to work out. Only once or twice did we end up having an event cancelled because there was a scheduling conflict. We had some venues where the crowd was huge but not every event worked the way we wanted it to.

There was the getting excited about an event that was set up, then walking into a room with barely anyone there. Not a lot of people came to some events, but the environment was right. The people who were there, were there to listen.

In your head, the crowd got bigger than it actually was.

In the end, it was the message that counted and whether there was a huge crowd there to hear it, or just a couple of people – that was all that was really important.

On Canada Day, July 1, 2008, in Thunder Bay, Ontario, I had the opportunity to talk to one of the largest crowds we had during Cycle to Walk.

Dream Big

✦

Early on we discovered that the word "rest" is a relative term.

The original plan had been to follow the pattern of Rick Hansen's Man in Motion Tour. He would travel for three days, take two off, travel one, take one off. Then start the schedule over again, but when we realized the average day not spent on the hand cycle wasn't really a rest day – we changed the name to "non-cycling days."

We also quickly realized that the number of days actually spent cycling was dictated more by where we had to be on certain days, how far we had to travel to reach that destination, the terrain and the accommodations we had each night and where they were located.

How long we stayed in communities was determined by the events or interviews that were planned in each place and, sometimes, the more mundane things we needed to get done.

Non-cycle days would be full of interviews, meetings or events for all of us. Any down time we had was spent by me writing my daily blog, Chris filing reports, talking to media or booking things to make sure I didn't have any spare time, Bertha doing laundry or going grocery shopping, Lynn or Carly cleaning up the motor home and Suburban and Doug dealing with issues from the head office in Whitehorse, maintaining the vehicles or planning the next cycling day.

A typical day of cycling would run something like this: After we had breakfast together I would be in my room finishing off my blog or sorting out my riding gear. When I was ready, I would sit and stare at the map, visualizing the coming day's travel. I was focused and determined to hand cycle to a specific community or a certain number of kilometers. It was important to me to establish what I felt the goal should be each day and then I would share it with the team.

The road crew took the motor home to the dump station to empty the sewage tanks, then to the gas station where they would fuel up and fill the water tank.

Doug would pick me up in the Suburban around 8:30 to drive to the point where we stopped cycling the night before or, depending upon how long we had been in any particular community, where we arrived a few days earlier. If we had media commitments, we usually fit them in before we started riding for the day. Events such as speaking to groups in communities were more often done at lunch or in the evenings after I finished cycling.

Before we left our starting point each morning my camel back was filled with a Gatorade/water combination, the GPS was attached to the back of the bike and I would get plugged into my MP3 to listen to music for the next four, six, eight, ten hours. I was stubborn about my music. I would keep the MP3 on even during rainy days. I went through three MP3s and four head sets because they would get wet and stop working. Or get tangled up in the hand cranks.

Then I would start riding measuring off one turn of the crank, one kilometer, one hour at a time. I always found the first 15 kilometers in the morning or right after lunch the most challenging. That's when I needed to mentally encourage myself the most.

The motor home would stay in front of me. Bertha and Carly or Lynn would drive a few kilometers ahead, wait for me to catch up, then leapfrog ahead another few kilometers. The Suburban, usually with Doug and Chris on board, would be behind me, but every once in a while they would pull out almost beside me to block off a freeway access ramp so I wouldn't get run over by people looking the wrong way while trying to merge into traffic.

When I wanted to stop for a bathroom break or snack I would raise my right arm in the air. Doug or Chris would radio ahead to the motor home, which would wait until I arrived and not leapfrog further down the road.

The inside walls of the motor home started to resemble a big notice board after a week or so on the road and occasionally someone would change the items stuck on the wall. There were photos of Doug, Bertha, myself and Chris – some were good pictures. Others not so flattering. Photos of the Whitehorse office staff, adults and children we encountered along the way. And some of the notable points we achieved along the way like border crossing and "welcome to our town" signs.

ONTARIO WEST

Manitoba to Marathon

June 20-July 12, 2008

There were hand written notes of encouragement from children we met.

"I hope you will raise lots of money for Polio, from Landon"

"I like you because you shared with us! Claudia"

A piece of boxboard with a quarter scotch taped to the center of it. *"Here's a donation for you, July 15, 2008, Turtle Creek Lodge, Lake Manitou"* I thought that one was great!

A piece of paper that referred to the amount of food I ate and Manitoba's provincial theme. *"I'm not hungry. I'm full of spirited energy!"*

An Irish prayer.

"May the road rise up to meet you
May the wind be always at your back
May the sun shine warm upon your face
And rains fall soft upon your fields
And until we meet again
My God hold you in the hollow of his hand."

Among all of those were brochures from Wheel to Walk, Run for One Planet and the Multifaith Walk Against Violence. If there wasn't anything else to do while in the motor home we could always just read the walls.

We added one item to our safety plan when we left Winnipeg. CB (citizen band) radios were installed so we could communicate with the many truck drivers that we expected to meet on the infamous Highway 17 in Northern Ontario.

As we rolled out of the prairies and into Ontario I decided that the one bug I did like was the dragonfly. The mosquitoes, black flies and everything else were hanging around trying to eat me. The dragonfly on the other hand swooped in and ate them. I'm truly grateful to them because, as much as the road crew supported me, I didn't see them hovering around me to eat bugs all day.

Kenora, Ontario, was hosting a street festival when we arrived and they gave us a parade into town, escorted by the police, a pipe band and six Corvettes. We spent an entertaining day at the park where we sold T-shirts, talked to people and spread the message. They also had a play about David Thomson –he explored Canada from Kenora to Rocky Mountain House in Alberta back in the days when exploring something literally meant no one else had ever been there – plus a concert by two pipe bands and a clog dancing group.

One of my presentations in Kenora was at the Ecole Ste. Margeurite Bourgeoys, a French immersion school. The kids had some great questions. They had the ability to cut through all the rhetoric and get right to the quick of their curiosity. It made me do some serious soul searching because I knew they would spot a pat answer if I gave one.

"Is it better for people to talk to you about your legs than it is for them to just stare at you?"

I'd start off by saying, "That's a great question. I think it's very important not to stare at people and ask questions if you're wondering why they're so different."

I gave the example of me being at the pool and people seeing my legs and how different they are. Some just stare. Others come up to me to ask about my legs and why. "Don't stare. Ask questions. Don't be afraid to ask questions rather than just staring and walking away. It's a natural part of behavior to look at things that are different and the size of my legs is different. When someone just stares and walks away I feel hurt, offended. But mostly I feel I'm being judged."

"Do you get tired of having a crutch all the time?"

I said, "'yes. There were days when I was tired and bitter about having crutches and braces. Going to school was tough. I was teased and picked on and it was always harder for me to fit in. But that changed when I went to India and saw what my life could have been. I began to truly appreciate what I have. Regardless of my disadvantages I can stand up on my own two feet."

"Why are you doing this?"

"I don't believe that anyone should be a Polio survivor. There shouldn't be any Polio and I'm doing this because we have to eradicate this disease while we have the chance. For most Canadians, Polio is an issue of the past. But it's still out there and we are still at risk. Polio does not discriminate, nor does it have any boundaries. It doesn't matter what religion you practice, where you were born or what role you play in your community."

When we signed up for Cycle to Walk, everyone had to agree that we wouldn't drink any alcohol at all for the duration of the trip. We were invited to a cocktail party on our last night in Kenora where they offered us a glass of wine when we arrived. Everyone would have liked to have a sip, but we stuck to our guns and had only water, pop or juice.

Thunder Bay, Ontario, was a very emotional place for me. There was, for me, a very special feeling in the air. It was my old college town. It was the beginning of my father's diocese. There were a lot of old friends there from both the church and the college. It was also the beginning of the infamous Highway 17, The Terry Fox Courage Highway, between Thunder Bay and Nipigon – a narrow winding two lane road with a lot of heavy transport truck traffic along the northern shore of Lake Superior. And knowing that it was here that Terry Fox ended his journey…

Things had changed since my last visit, but I'd arrived at Kakabeka Falls Provincial Park, just west of Thunder Bay, with the love of my life – my 27-speed hand cycle and the message of Cycle to Walk. This is one of the best places to be with the love of your life. The area is very romantic. The falls are beautiful and it has great camping.

As a teenager I thought the true love of my life with me at Kakabeka Falls would be Elizabeth Soloway. Now, as an adult, it's my hand cycle. Funny how things change.

Confederation College provided rooms for the entire road team. I didn't get my old room back although I did see it. It was a lot cleaner than I remember.

It was great to see the support from the college. The emotional support. The involvement, providing us accommodations and volunteering for events. Financial support. The student union, where I was president for the 2000-2001 school year, gave us a donation for $5,000. I met with college president Pat Lang and she matched the student's contribution on behalf of the college.

We talked about how college graduates can give back to their local community. It's wonderful that a college recognizes an alumni bringing attention to a global community issue.

My first night in Thunder Bay was one of those rare experiences – a break from the campaign. I went bowling and played mini-golf with some friends. I didn't fare very well with either and learned that I really should stick to hand cycling. Then we went to a movie – something I haven't been able to do for months.

When we walked into the bowling alley an employee, Meghan Rawson, shouted at me "You're early." I asked her what she meant and she told me she was a fan of Cycle to Walk, had been following our progress on the web site and we had arrived in Thunder Bay a day earlier than scheduled. Later, when we were having dinner, our host Taylor welcomed me to Thunder Bay and he was a big fan of Cycle to Walk as well.

It's great to have a champion for your cause in the community. Reverend Paul Carr established an event coordinating committee which combined Rotarians, church and community leaders. They worked for months organizing special events in Thunder Bay and Nipigon.

All the Anglican churches in Thunder Bay declared June 29 to be Cycle to Walk Sunday. We went from church to church to church all day long. Each visit was short but worth the time to see the tremendous support. The congregations had been preparing for months for our arrival. Their bulletin boards were covered with my blog entries, polio statistics, pictures and route maps. They had sit-down lunches or barbeques going all day long. The entire offering from each church was donated to Cycle to Walk.

At St. Paul's Anglican Church, Reverend Debra Kraft had a "Listening Together" time for the children who were at the service. That Sunday, her message was unfinished work. She had a toothbrush and used it on her bottom teeth only, then said she had finished the job. They talked about taking on a task and completing it – in this case, also brushing the top teeth. Then she related that lesson to Cycle to Walk. Not just the physical part, the journey to Cape Spear, but also to our message about the eradication of Polio.

Her sermon was equally powerful, about "God is Love" and related that to the feeling she got from me and my road crew. She is one powerful speaker and you can see she lives what she preaches.

I also met Dave Shannon, a most inspirational man. He was the first and, as far as I know, the only quadriplegic to cross Canada, in 1997, by electric wheelchair to promote empowerment for disenfranchised communities and greater social inclusion for all Canadians. It was great to hear from a pioneer in creating awareness of the need to provide access and facilities for those with mobility issues. Now, just about every public building and office building in Canada provides accessible entrances. I hope that Cycle to Walk has the same impact on Canadians.

No, I didn't ask him where he found an electrical extension cord long enough to stretch from coast to coast.

I was 28 years old and Cycle to Walk was in Thunder Bay for my 25th Canada Day celebration. We had a scrumptious breakfast with Reverend Nancy and Bill Ringham. Then we were joined by church members, Rotary clubs and the Thunder Bay Cycling Club for the ride into the city. There was so much support. As we approached the outskirts there were people honking their horns for us and lining the sides of the road to clap and cheer.

Allon Reddoch was there to share it with us. He, Chris and Carly handed out Cycle to Walk wrist bands – these were blue elasticized wrist bands with the campaign name impressed into them. We didn't know how well they would be received when the idea was first suggested back in Whitehorse, but we noticed that people put them on and kept them on when we handed them out. Doug drove the SUV. Bertha combined dancing in her seat with driving the motor home.

After the parade I was invited to the main stage at Marina Park to talk about Polio and Cycle to Walk. It was the largest number of people I had ever talked to. When I was finished people came to our tent all day to give donations, buy T-shirts and get their pinkies died purple. Their enthusiasm sure gave us a lift!

Our last non-cycling day in Thunder Bay brought us to the residents of St. Joseph's Care Group, the Ontario March of Dimes and the Fort William and the Thunder Bay and District Rotary Club. At each I spoke before Polio survivors and they told us stories of the fear of the 1950s. This campaign brought out a lot of those people and their histories.

I think we touched every age group. The older generations remembered the horrors of the past. For the younger generations, who didn't have that experience, the goal of Cycle to Walk was to spread the power of turning a dream into reality, overcoming obstacles and what can happen when one is persistent, determined, focused and supported. What a community can do for a dream.

Emotionally, the day we left Thunder Bay was probably one of the most difficult of the entire trip. Not only were we leaving a community that had been my stomping ground for three years, we were leaving a place that was very receptive to our message and supported our cause without reservation. If a community can embrace you, Thunder Bay had not only hugged us, they gave us a big kiss.

We took time to honor one of the men who has always been one of my personal heroes. When I met Rick Hansen a year or so ago, I was thrilled to meet the Man In Motion. But I was equally thrilled to meet someone who had actually known Terry Fox.

To me, Terry is the epitome of hope, courage, determination and selflessness. When people compared my journey to his or to Rick Hansen's, I was deeply honored, humbled by and indebted to those people who set such a high standard for us to try and achieve.

We rode east from Thunder Bay to the Terry Fox monument. Amanda Nelson, Lee Anne Jessiman and Nancy Ringham lead a short memorial for Terry and shared some of their thoughts about Cycle to Walk and sacrifices that were being made. I thought of Bertha and Doug putting their lives on hold for half a year just to be here with me. Carly spending this time with us solely because of our friendship. My godmother Lynn. Everyone on this team made sacrifices because we had faith in this cause.

People I went to church camp with. Parishioners from the Thunder Bay churches. They all supported the campaign and talked about what it meant to them. They were quite emotional, speaking about how one person can give so much of him or herself to draw attention to an issue that needs to be addressed. They said they were proud. That I was their hero too. Lots of comparisons to Terry and the respect for what he did.

I chose not to talk at that event. Terry is so much of a hero of mine and, that hill top where his monument stands, that's his space and the time we spent there was his time. I felt that if I talked, that would overstep the respect held for what he did. I sat in silence, reflected upon the campaign and said thank you to him. I listened this day to what the others had to say.

I remembered his words. Like most of us, he wasn't a gifted public speaker. He couldn't motivate a crowd by his oratory alone. It was his actions that inspired people. However he did have the ability to come up with the right words at the right time.

"Dreams are made if people only try.

I believe in miracles…

I have to…

Because somewhere the hurting must stop."

I placed a dollar at the base of the post that marks his final step. His goal was to raise one dollar for each Canadian to help fund cancer research. Then it was time to move on.

Nipigon, at the far end of a beautiful day for cycling along the Terry Fox Highway of Courage, is Carly's home town. People lined the streets in their work clothes – nursing scrubs and garage coveralls to cheer us through. Times were tough in Nipigon. Their mill had burned down in 2007 and a lot of people lost their jobs. It was inspirational to receive so much support from a town that had lost so much.

It was also only 89 kilometers away from the mid point of the cycle across Canada. The actual halfway was in Schreiber, just a short uphill ride away that made me feel like I had been climbing cliffs all day long.

I rode past a little bit of history when we passed through White River, Ontario. This was the town where, in 1914, a bear cub was purchased by Lieutenant Harry Coleburn – who named the bear Winnie after his hometown of Winnipeg – and who hasn't read A.A. Milne's Winnie the Pooh books? The topic of discussion in the motor home was about nothing else for two days. Carly and I are young enough to remember the books. Doug and Bertha, I think, are approaching second childhood and will have to read them again to their increasing number of grandchildren.

Then there's Montreal River – which isn't a really big river, but it has a really big hill. It's written about in Terry Fox's biographies and it's a big part of the movie that was made about his Marathon of Hope. It has a great downhill, but you have to climb up to make use of it. I actually wondered as I was cruising downhill on the east side how Terry would have felt going up. I pictured that look of agony on his face as he ran and decided it must be here that image comes from.

When I was growing up in Sault Ste Marie, Ontario, I always had to stay at a friend's house when my parents went out of town. This time my parents were in England for the Lambeth Conference – where all the Anglican bishops of the world get together every 10 years for meetings – and now I got to stay in the house while they're out. I must have finally grown up!

They left a sign on the door welcoming the team, keys for everyone and a gift certificate to one of my favorite restaurants. In exchange for this, we only had to do the dishes, water the plants and make sure the recycle was taken out to the curb – no, I'm kidding! It was nice to be back in comfortable, familiar surroundings.

The house had been built in 1876 for the Anglican bishop and in 2008 was still serving that purpose. I knew my father was planning to retire in September so, when I walked into the house that it would for be the last time.

We took a couple of days off in 'the Soo' and I took advantage of that to show the team members my town and go to a couple of my old favorite eating places. Mrs. B's Pizza. The West Side Café for poutine – I did this one on my own because I didn't want anyone on the campaign to know that I ate anything other than healthy food. I was also far enough away from my dietician, Laura Wilson in Whitehorse, there was no way she could ever find out. Boy, did that poutine ever taste good!

The churches arranged a community cycle between St. James Anglican Church and St. Mark's in Heyden. Two other cyclists, Rick Falls and Fiona Ortiz, joined me for the ride. My brother Matt, who had just returned from New Zealand with his wife Lynda, also rode with me for part of the way. As we got closer to St. Mark's, it looked like there was a picket line in front of the building, but it turned out to be people holding up signs saying "Stamp out Polio!" and "Go Ramesh!"

We joined up with the city mascot, Bon Soo, to ride in the Rotaryfest parade. It was a massive parade. The biggest one we ever participated in. There were thousands of people there, a lot of them familiar faces for me. Old high school classmates. Neighbours. Church members. And some new faces, like kids from the Children's Rehabilitation Centre where I spoke earlier, and those "picketers" from St. Marks with their signs once again.

Two friends of mine were getting married while I was there, Sarah and Morty Walls. I was one of the guests and – on a day that was supposed to be about the bride and groom – they stood up, talked about Cycle to Walk and encouraged their guests to support our cause. I was completely floored by their kindness that, for me, showed that no matter what we are doing in life, we must all come together for causes that affect all of our lives in varying ways.

My feelings leaving Sault Ste. Marie were much as they had been when we left Thunder Bay, but there was such a finality to the act of departure. This was closure for me. I knew that with my dad retiring, I would lose connection to many of these people and places. Cycle to Walk brought me to Bishophurst – the name of the house where we lived – one last time and now it was time to leave.

Bertha kept telling me there are no coincidences – just God-directed paths to take. One of those paths took us to Peachy's restaurant in Elliot Lake.

Elliot Lake, Ontario, was actually a bit off our route but that's where we thought we might find accommodations for the night so, after ending the riding day, we loaded up the bike and headed north. As we drove into town we saw people cleaning garbage from the ditches. Bertha tooted her horn and waved as we drove by and they waved back.

After Chris and I got settled into our rooms – Chris needed a room so he could finish his daily reports and use the wireless system to email them to Whitehorse – I headed down to the restaurant. There was the local Rotary club, having a pizza and beer dinner after spending the day on their highway clean-up project. They were delighted to see me. One of the women saw my presentation to Rotary in Sault Ste. Marie and, after seeing our vehicle on the road, told the other members about the campaign. Then I walked in the door.

I was really tired that day, we had cycled just over a hundred kilometers, but they asked me to give them a presentation – so I did and between themselves, they collected about $450 for Cycle to Walk.

Coincidence? I don't think so.

There were a lot of different vehicles along this stretch of road. On one hill a woman in her fifties, with an old style of bike loaded down with gear, passed me easily. The road crew hadn't let me forget just how slow I was going. Going up a hill just outside of Espanola, Ontario, I spotted a horse and buggy ahead of me. I made it my goal to pass them before the top and just before the top of the rise, I did. It's not every day I can say I won a race against a horse and buggy, even if I was the only one racing.

We swung south, onto Manitoulin Island and caught a ferry across the main channel between Lake Superior and Georgian Bay, from South Baymouth to Tobermory. The captain let me think I was piloting the ship for a couple of seconds but my nerves told me that, no matter how neat it may have felt to steer, this wasn't something I should be doing. Being in danger of getting run over on my hand cycle seemed so much less intimidating. Doug gave me five dollars to buy a snack at the cafeteria and I returned with the change - $120 thanks to all the people who came to speak with me and donate.

Because of traffic concerns we didn't ride into Toronto, Ontario, but actually swung north of Lake Simcoe. In Thornbury we stayed with Reid and Mary Asselstine, Rotarians who had gone to India three years ago with the Global Initiative for the eradication of Polio. "When I was putting a drop into a young child's mouth, "he told us, "a Rotarian's wife looked at me and said, 'Reid. That one will walk.' And that's so important."

Salk Street is on the grounds of Sanofi-Pasteur in Toronto, Ontario. The facility, formerly called Connaught Medical Research Laboratories, was instrumental in enabling scientists to manufacture bulk quantities of vaccine.

Do You Take Donations?

✦

We all do different jobs and every day we go to our work place and we wonder if what we are doing is actually having an impact on the people we are serving.

The Polio vaccine manufacturers must have those thoughts. They live in a country where they don't see Polio or the effects of Polio. They are working every day on a vaccination that doesn't seem to have value in their world.

The Vaccines Division of Sanofi Pasteur was, for myself, the most important part of Toronto we went to. They are the world's largest supplier of vaccines…not just for Polio but for other preventable diseases as well, like diphtheria, meningitis and flus …and they welcomed us with open arms. Even in the parking lot when we arrived.

Doug asked them where we could park the vehicles. Cities like Toronto just aren't set up to accommodate motor homes or Suburbans towing trailers. Usually they would direct us to the back of the parking lot or tell us there wasn't enough room, you can unload here but go park somewhere else. But there, the attendant just looked at Doug and said "Park wherever you like."

We were given pass tags and escorted to the conference room where lunch was served. The vice-president, Luis Barreto, asked each of us how we got involved in the campaign. Then I told my story and made a short presentation. After that he had some of his corporate officers, Shawn

Gilchrist, Christopher Rutty – a Polio historian I've talked to on the phone in the past, Michael Schunk and Nancy Simpson, introduce themselves and tell us what they did in the company. We got a lesson in how the first vaccines were developed and then produced on a large scale. Bertha told me later that she got the impression we were being sized up to see how we could fit in with what they are doing and she thought there may be discussion in their board room after we left about where they might go with it.

After we finished Cycle to Walk I received an invitation from Sanofi to speak to their employees in the fall of 2009.

They took us on a tour of the facility and out to the building where the actual Polio vaccine is made. We weren't allowed into the laboratory or manufacturing area because of the fear of contamination, but they did provide us a very detailed explanation of how it works. I felt overwhelmed, knowing just how great an international effort had been made and was still being made.

Later we walked on Salk Street, near where Dr. Jonas Salk did his field trials and where Sanofi Pasteur is located. I kept thinking, "It all began and still begins right here!"

Luis told me that "when" I return, I would be taken through the secure area. Then there were more photos taken and they wished us well on our travels.

I think I did remind them that what they're doing is important. That it is making a difference because we are so close – not just because of the people in the front lines who are administering the vaccine, but because of people like themselves who manufacture it.

We also visited Ontario's lieutenant governor, David Onley, and I saw the future. David is a Polio survivor. He got it as a child. His legs are paralyzed and he uses a scooter rather than crutches to get around. I think I would like to get one of those one day. It was pretty neat and he used it to go everywhere and do everything. We expected only a photo opportunity and that did happen. But when the photographers left he asked us to sit down and talk about the campaign.

It was very inspirational spending time with him. He is a role model of how someone with mobility issues can remain positive. Stay focused on strengths and abilities rather than weaknesses and disabilities to become successful leaders within the community. Like Franklin Roosevelt, he sees what can be done, not what should be done.

He also issued a very public statement to the media about a parent's responsibility to their children to ensure they receive the vaccine.

"While the vast majority of current polio cases occur in distant countries where polio is still endemic, in this age of casual jet travel between continents, Canadians cannot afford to be complacent when it comes to having our children vaccinated."

I'm not a big baseball fan but I could turn into one. The Toronto Blue Jays got involved with Cycle to Walk. We were asked to be part of the pregame activities before they played the Oakland Athletics on the evening of August 5. I went down onto the field with the hand cycle and stood beside third base while they introduced me and mentioned the Cycle to Walk campaign over the intercom system.

I wasn't nervous about going onto the field. I was more nervous that someone might ask me a baseball question. I hadn't followed baseball for years and didn't know who the players were or what their position was. Just before I went out to the field I learned that Cito Gaston - he won two World Series championships with this club while I was just a kid – was returning to be the manager of the Jays. But I didn't know where he was returning from!

When I saw him I told him "Welcome back."

"Thanks for supporting the Jays," he responded, then presented me with a Blue Jays game uniform with my name stitched across the back above the number. I just crossed my fingers and hoped he wouldn't ask me a baseball question.

When I rode the bike off the field. I don't remember if there was much of a reaction, but Bertha told me she thought the crowd was quite warm in their acknowledgement.

It was a pretty good game too, and Toronto won in the bottom of the ninth inning. I was thinking they should invite me back more often because we've been to two baseball games on this trip and the home team won each time.

When we got back to our accommodations at Wycliffe College the receptionist showed us that we were on the front page of 'Metro Toronto' – the free newspaper that is handed out to every passenger on Toronto subway and city bus routes -and there was a photo and article in the Toronto Star.

After leaving Toronto we spent a day cycling into Peterborough, Ontario – where I'm sure every person, pet and passer-by must now know about Cycle to Walk.

All of the police escorts we had through the entire journey were very good. For most of them it was just a job. For others – like the escort we had through Quebec City, it was something to enjoy. To be a part of. For Dan Gemmiti, who was our escort driver in Peterborough, it apparently was a passion. He cranked up the siren and the lights on his

ONTARIO EAST

Marathon to Quebec border

July 13 - August 15, 2008

car and made sure everyone in the city - who had the ability to hear - knew who we were, where we were and where we were going. His wife Jill and their two daughters rode in the car with him.

I don't know if it was his siren call that summoned everyone, but the mayor Paul Ayotte and the Rotary district governor, Tom Bennett and a whole lot of other people were at the Holiday Inn to greet us when we arrived.

Just before I went to bed that night I called my dad, who had returned to Canada after his conference in England, and found out that I was an uncle. My sister Jill and her husband Aaron had just given birth to a boy, Holden Parker.

It seems odd now, but given where we were and what we were doing at the time, it makes sense. The very first thought that went through my head when I heard the news was that they won't think twice about ensuring my little nephew will receive his three doses of the vaccine, which are needed at two months, four months and six months!

A couple of days later my vantage point, sitting low on the hand cycle where I can look a car bumper straight in the eye, gave me a clue we were moving east. I started seeing fewer and fewer Toronto Maple Leaf license plates and more for the Ottawa Senators.

We were all astounded when we realized that we had been on the road for four months upon reaching Ottawa, and two of those months had been spent crossing Ontario. It was also a sad moment for us because Carly had to head back home. When we left Ottawa, she returned to Nipigon. She left us with wonderful memories of her singing and the fact that she was the only person to get the motor home stuck. She parked on the side of the road one day and found the highway had soft shoulders. It took the Ontario Provincial Police to pull us out and get us moving again.

Allon was in Ottawa to greet us. He was on his way to the Canadian Medical Association's annual general meeting in Quebec City and the timing was perfect for him to fly from Whitehorse a few days early to be in Ottawa when we arrived.

The Yukon's Member of Parliament, Larry Bagnall, lined up a full day for us on Parliament Hill. He arranged parking for us so we could drive right onto the grounds and leave the vehicles for the day. We watched the changing of the guard on the lawn in front of the Parliament buildings, then met up with him for a personal tour of the Center Block.

We were allowed to pull the bike around behind us while we walked through the building and used it as a prop for taking pictures when I sat in the Speaker's Chair in the House of Commons with the road crew gathered around me. I also got to sit in the chair reserved for the Prime Minister.

As luck would have it the Speaker of the House, Peter Milliken, was in his office and had us in for an impromptu visit. He had a lot of stories about his predecessors in that office, including the only Yukoner who ever occupied the speaker's position – George Black. Apparently there are a lot of rabbits on the Parliament grounds and Black liked taking shots at them with a .22 handgun aimed through his office window. When there was a complaint lodged against him, he allegedly took a shot at the plaintiff in the hallway just outside the office. The scar made by the bullet, which Larry showed us, is still in the woodwork very close to where the official portrait of George Black can keep an eye on it.

We had pictures taken with the Speaker in front of the wall where the photographer Josef Karsh took the famous photo of Winston Churchill. He had been trying to get the right picture all day and it hadn't worked. He asked Churchill to remove his cigar. Churchill refused, so Karsh walked over and pulled it out of his mouth. As Churchill glared at him, he took the picture.

Larry took us to Liberal leader Stephane Dion's office where we had an opportunity to sit down and talk to him about Cycle to Walk. He was interested in sitting on the bike but we discouraged him because he was wearing a suit and the chain grease would get all over him.

"It takes a lot of commitment and courage to undertake such a journey" he told me after assuring me that his party was fully behind the Global Polio Eradication Initiative, then spread his hands indicating an increasing distance, "but you picked the largest country in the world in which to do it." Second largest country in the world actually, but I didn't correct him.

Later in the afternoon we heard that Prime Minister Stephen Harper had agreed to meet us the next morning. That, Bertha told me, was why she insisted I bring a sports coat and pants.

There was much debate over what I should wear to meet the Prime Minister. Should I put on the coat and pants or should I wear shorts so he can see my legs and understand what Polio can do. It still hadn't been resolved by the next morning. I called Val Royle in Whitehorse to ask her opinion. It was early in Ottawa so it was still the middle of the night in Whitehorse.

Val's husband, Jaime, was quite polite considering the hour. He told me that Val was actually in Anchorage, Alaska – where it was even earlier in the morning or later at night, depending upon your perspective – and gave me the number at her hotel. When Val answered the phone, she was quite nice too.

"Well," she told me, "You don't want to out-dress the Prime Minister. Do whatever Allon thinks." Then I assume she hung up and went back to sleep. In the end it was the sports coat and pants. The Prime Minister and I wore pretty much the same thing.

We didn't have to go through any metal screening devices to get in, which is good because I can imagine the noise the metal in my braces and crutch as well as the hand cycle would have made, but we did have to pass through some very special plexiglass doors. We all had to show picture identification – which I didn't have, but fortunately Bertha did have my passport in her purse – what are road mothers for!

I was glad we didn't have to leave her behind when we entered the building. We had been told we could only have some of the team members with us. So Carly, Chris, Bertha, Allon and I got to go in.

Stephen Harper looks in person much like he does on television. He has a very nice smile and seemed genuinely interested in meeting us.

He mostly listened as I told him about Cycle to Walk and later we both talked about the Global Polio Eradication Initiative and Canada's role in it. When I mentioned Afghanistan and expressed my dream that the Taliban might stop fighting for one day, allow the vaccinations to go ahead and save the lives of thousands of children, he just smiled.

"The Taliban," he told me, "are anti-everything good. They are against all programs and government." It was, he assured me, an almost impossible situation.

When we left his office we drove out to a restaurant for lunch. While we were eating the waitress, Marie-Claire, came back to the table and asked us what Cycle to Walk was about. I told her that we were spreading the message about Polio eradication and rehabilitation.

"Do you take donations?" she asked me. Then reached into her belt, pulled out twenty dollars and handed it to me. "My dad had Polio," she explained.

Our last day in Ottawa I went for a ride along the Rideau Canal with a teacher, Deirdre, who told me she had recently been in Guyana where she witnessed first-hand the reality for many Polio survivors who must crawl to get around. When she saw the Cycle to Walk trailer she got excited and wanted to tour me through Ottawa and along the canal. As we cycled past the Tomb of the Unknown Soldier several people stopped us to talk about Cycle to Walk.

Before she left she told me she was going to introduce her students to the purple pinkie project to help increase Polio awareness. When we left Ottawa, I had the feeling that we were having an impact. Even if we didn't get many donations, people like Marie Claire and Deirdre were going to carry our message beyond our short encounters. Even if none of the politicians reached into their pockets and made personal contributions, they were in positions where their decisions could make an even greater contribution to the eradication of Polio.

A couple of days later I was crossing a bridge over the Ottawa River and halfway across the signage turned from English into French and just like that, we were in Quebec.

Again God was working for us in mysterious ways. One of the problems we had while approaching Quebec was that we couldn't find a French-speaking coordinator in Whitehorse who could donate the amount of time required to help us arrange events and media coverage. The board and the road crew had already determined that we would get through Quebec as best we could without any expectations of much happening.

Then into the Whitehorse office, a few days before we entered "La Belle Province", walked Helene Beaulieu. She had just moved from Quebec to Whitehorse and was looking for work. In the meantime she had heard we needed a francophone to help coordinate activities in Quebec. Not only did she know how to speak French, she knew who to speak it to. In the end Helene was only able to help us for about two weeks before she did get a real job, but those two weeks were invaluable.

Right from the first day, when the town of LaChute greeted us until we entered New Brunswick our calendar was full. There were even events that weren't events! While I was riding east of Maskinonge several hundred motorcycles passed us heading in the opposite direction. I've never seen so many motor cycles at one time in my life. Most of them honked and waved, gave a thumbs-up or shouted encouragement as they whizzed by.

While we were in Berthierville, just east of Montreal, two busloads of young army cadets stopped to stretch their legs in the parking lot of the hotel we were staying at. Recognizing an opportunity when it presented itself, I asked the adult officer accompanying them if I could talk to the cadets. She agreed and provided translation while I spoke. It was the first time I had to work with a translator for my presentation, so I kept it really short. Just long enough to get the message across I think. I don't speak French so I don't know exactly what she said, but it got a positive reaction from the kids.

We drove into Montreal the next day. Boy, am I glad I didn't cycle! The traffic was insane. Most people were pretty patient with the country folk from the Yukon but we did get honked at more than once. The only thing that saved us from getting lost in the maze of streets and alleged freeways getting in and out of downtown to where we were staying in Laval was the Garmin global positioning guidance system in the Suburban. The voice of "Madame Garmin" might be really irritating, but the instructions were accurate – until we got on a new road that wasn't in the programming, then she panicked and tried to get us on a road she knew.

There were several radio and newspaper interviews downtown, a police escorted ride through Laval with the CATAL retired cyclists club and a dinner with all the Rotary clubs in Laval, so we used Madame Garmin a lot and managed to get where we needed to be when we needed to be there.

We also met with Francine Senecal, the vice-president of the Montreal Executive Committee for Sports and Recreation in city hall. She was very welcoming, telling me that "your determination and dedication are an inspiration to all of us. Your presence in Montreal also reminds us that Polio can still strike in Canada. I hope that Canadians all along your route will become aware of the cause you hold so close to your heart and give generously to Cycle to Walk."

Then she let me ride the hand cycle right there on the marble floors and between the marble pillars of city hall. I don't imagine a lot of other cyclists have been able to take a spin in there.

Many of the world's ten to twenty million Polio survivors don't have access to the simplest of rehabilitative devices like braces and crutches. There are still a lot places where people, who do have access to brace and crutches, still find they can't go and things they can't do because the services or the building or lack of public education stops them from doing so.

When we reached Trois Rivieres, Quebec, about halfway between Montreal and Quebec City right on the St. Lawrence River, we were to participate in their second annual Accessibility Awareness Day. This was an event where people with hearing, sight, speech or mobility issues would test to see how accessible some places were for them. But we, the people who actually have the issues, weren't the ones testing the facilities or services.

We were there to observe as perfectly healthy people were given specific handicaps, then told to perform certain tasks.

Doug had to navigate narrow sidewalks and try to enter shops in a wheelchair. Then he had to walk into a restaurant blindfolded and ask for a table for two. Chris had to wear ear plugs, to simulate a hearing loss, then go into the tourism information office and ask for a map. He also had to try to work an ATM machine while down on his knees and holding his arms close to his body, to simulate a child or very short person.

It was a good experience for everyone since it gave mobile people like Doug and Chris the experience of what it would be like if they ever lose any aspect of it.

As I approached Quebec City on the Chemin du Roy – The King's Highway – one of the most scenic roads in all of Canada with what seemed to be the highest concentration of heavy equipment and road construction sites on earth – Jean Marc, a cyclist just out for his afternoon exercise pulled up beside me to ask what Cycle to Walk was. I told him about spreading our message and why I was doing it.

QUEBEC
NEW BRUNSWICK

August 15-September 6, 2008

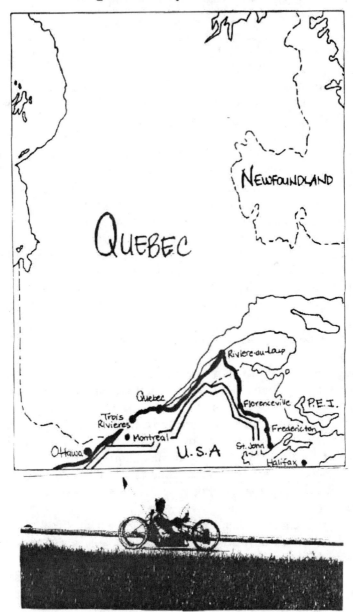

"The last time I ran with someone doing this kind of thing," he proudly told me, "was with Terry Fox. I ran marathons back then. I ride bikes now. I was about 25 or 26 when he was here. He wasn't even recognized until he reached Montreal and Toronto. I didn't know who he was then but I ran with him in Quebec City." He thanked me for riding for Polio and told me it meant a lot for him to be here on the road with me.

We rode together for a short distance until I got too slow on the hills then he bid me adieu and headed off down the road. I wonder if he'll have the Terry Fox story and now, my story, to tell to the next cross country fund raiser that he meets on the road.

It was the beginning of a pattern of being compared to or encountering people who met Terry Fox. For me, it was more than an honor to be recognized in the same catagory as a man who accomplished so much. His run never got to western Canada so people there never had the experience. In eastern Canada, there seems to be many who encountered him on the road – usually by chance, sometimes by design – who have never forgotten the time they shared.

Later in the day, after we had arrived in Quebec and were loading the hand cycle into the trailer there was an elderly man in a wheelchair sitting in a doorway close to our vehicles. It turned out that he was a Polio survivor and his history told me much about how endemic Polio really was before the vaccines and how some myths have persisted through time.

"I got it (Polio) from my mother," he told me, "She was in a wheelchair too."

We were supposed to meet the mayor the next day but instead we were introduced to a city councilor, Lisette Lapage, who was very nice but didn't really seem to understand why we were there. A second city councilor, Andre Demers, came into the office.

"This isn't one of the assignments I had today but I really wanted to meet you," he said, grabbing my shoulder and pumping my hand, "I'm a Polio survivor also." He took a close look at 'Little Brace' and told me that it was similar to the one he had at age one, but they didn't have fiberglass in their braces back then – just metal and leather.

We took the rest of the day off to explore this beautiful 400-year-old city. I went to have lunch with Kawina Robichaud, who was visiting Quebec. She was the Yukon artist who donated the silk screen painting to Cycle to Walk that we turned into our poster. Chris went to meet up with a girl that he remembered having a 'crush' on back in high school. Doug and Bertha went for a walk through the old city.

The night was filled with people. As part of their 400th anniversary celebrations, Quebec City was hosting a series of free concerts on the Plains of Abraham. A week earlier Paul McCartney had played to about a quarter of million people. The night we were there Celine Dion and a number of other Quebec performers were putting on a performance. About half the city must have congregated on the Plains.

The newspaper the next day said there were 300,000 there. It was a great concert! They sang mostly traditional Quebecois songs rather than the big hits and the crowd was crazy.

Even there, in the middle of all the music and excitement, I couldn't shake the message. I wondered how many of the people there had received the vaccine and, after seeing the rows upon rows of portable outhouses on the way in, how many were practicing good hygiene. The concert was a perfect example of how hundreds of thousands could come in contact with the Poliovirus in one evening. All it takes is one carrier not washing their hands.

We had one of the best police escorts a person could ask for early the next morning. Two constables, Martin Ferland and Carl Deschenes, had been up most of the night patrolling the concert and directing traffic. But there they were early the next morning, ready to guide us through the city to the ferry that would take us across the St. Lawrence River to the town of Levis.

The route was absolutely amazing! There were steep climbs and downhills, sharp corners, cobblestone streets and 400-year-old buildings. They led us over the curb and off the road onto the square in front of the Chateau Frontenac Hotel and stopped for pictures. When we reached the ferry, rather than just leaving because their duty was done, the two officers came on board and posed for photos with me.

They were so excited to be part of Cycle to Walk and that helped me because, just like them, I hadn't gotten a lot of sleep the night before either.

I did have the opportunity to speak at one church in the old city – at the Anglican Cathedral of the Holy Trinity. The congregation was very receptive and stayed for a long time after the service was over to talk with us. One woman told me she had contracted Polio at age eleven. Doctors suspected she got it while in a large public space at the Toronto Exhibition – which today is called the Canadian National Exhibition. It reminded me of my thoughts during the concert and just how lucky Canadians are today to have access to the vaccine.

The Quebec City International Festival of Military Bands was held while we were there. Rather than the standard organ music at the church service, we had the Band of the Corps of the Royal Electrical and Mechanical Engineers playing at the church service. The music was beautiful and they played an extra set when the service was over.

Later we watched more bands in front of the Chateau Frontenac - in the same spot we took pictures on the hand cycle the day before - then hired a horse and carriage to take us on a short tour. We draped the Cycle to

Walk banner over the back of the carriage so we could continue spreading the message.

The south shore of the St. Lawrence River is beautiful and there was a lot less traffic. I was cycling down the road and suddenly this big, unshaven guy in shorts and a T-shirt ran out in front of me and tried to direct me into his driveway. I stopped cycling and looked back at the Suburban wondering, "Who is this guy!?"

He had all these things stuck in his front yard. Cars with tires that turned in the wind. Planes with propellers that spun. It turned out this was our billet for the night. I looked at the place. It was an older house, about 120 years old actually, looked more than a little run down and I thought, "Oh my Gosh. We're going to be staying here!?"

It turned out that it wasn't only his home, it was also his business. He was advertising his wares with all the wind toys stuck in his front yard. He sold the stuff. But we didn't know that until later and he turned out to be a really cool guy. Cooked us a great meal that night then he and his wife made a fabulous breakfast the next morning. He is apparently the largest kite wholesaler in North America and took us on a tour of his warehouse and storefront. When we left he gave me a fish windsock.

In Riviere-du-Loup, the map showed a short route through the edge of the town. It looked pretty simple until we turned the corner and saw the hill. It was short, but it was straight up – an 18 degree slope according to the sign we found halfway up. That was the steepest and toughest climb I have ever made in my entire life. The hand cycle would roll backward every once in a while and it took everything I had to keep it going forward and get to the top. Even when I felt I couldn't do this any more, there was no other choice. The only thing between me and the bottom of the hill was hand cranking all the way to the top.

At the top, I was frustrated and tired. It wasn't anyone's fault that I had to go up that hill. Before we actually saw it nobody knew it was there and it had been my decision to take that route. I had to take it out on someone, so I took it out on Doug. He was frustrated and tired too so it blew up into an argument that ended up with neither of us talking to the other for the rest of the day. We even rode in separate vehicles so we wouldn't have to see one another.

Over a six month period there's always going to be some sort of dissent. A few times Chris and I could barely talk to one another. Doug and I occasionally blew off steam at each other, but nothing like that day in Riviere-du-Loup. Bertha and I never really had a falling out. How can you get mad at your mother? But she did straighten me out every once in a while when I deserved it.

In the end all the little things that unnessecarily blew up into big issues were kept in context by everyone. Sometimes it just took a time out – a cooling period. Other times it had to be resolved quietly, but it's hard to apologize – even when you're wrong, you still think you're right. In the end, nobody lost sight of the goal and the message.

Riding in the rain wasn't a lot of fun. I got covered by mud and dirt flying up from my own wheels and vehicles driving by. It reminded me that nobody should be condemned to living in the dirt.

Every Great Dream

✦

I think one of the highlights of reaching the Maritime provinces was the realization that the message was reaching beyond the borders of Canada. In Halifax, Nova Scotia, I was given a news article about Cycle to Walk printed in a newspaper from Hong Kong, China.

Another was comprehending that the people we were reaching, the younger generations of Canadians who need to learn what Polio is and what risk it poses to our future, were starting to understand why I was out there on my hand cycle. There are three and a half million Canadian children who are at risk today because they haven't been vaccinated. People were always ready to accept there are problems in India or Afghanistan, but they don't realize there's risk in Canada also. All it takes is one infected person arriving on a plane and it will be back.

Take a look at what happened with the H1N1 flu in April (2009). It started in Mexico and within days international travel had carried it as far away as New Zealand and Israel. It would take six months to develop a vaccine, but the virus was around the globe in less than a week!

One young man ran up beside me while I was cycling up a hill near Port Hawkesbury, Nova Scotia.

"Hey. Nice Bike!"

"Do you know why I'm biking?"

"No."

"Do you see my legs?"

"Yeh."

"What do you think of them?"

"Small."

"Why do you think that is?"

"I don't know."

"It's because I had a disease called Polio because I didn't receive a vaccination like you did when you were young."

This is all happening as I'm cycling and he's running uphill, so we're both a little out of breath. I learned his name, Christian. His age, eleven. I know I connected because later that night, while I was checking my email, I got a note from him saying "I think what you're doing is amazing. Good job!" I don't think he would have sent a message if I had just been some guy riding a hand cycle.

Spreading the word one hand crank, one day, one person, one community, one country at a time.

It's important for people to understand that an effort – Polio eradication – this big can't solely be the responsibility of just one major service organization like Rotary International. It takes a community. We must take it as our own cause even though we may not be personally involved. We have an obligation to care for others both in our own country and the global community because that's what we live in and we can't move somewhere else.

I found it nice to be able to talk in churches because, when you look at a church, it encompasses so many levels of community. For instance Christ Church Cathedral in Fredericton, New Brunswick, had the Olympic community, the school age community, religious leaders of several faiths, Rotarians, politicians, immigrants, Polio survivors.

Public education is how it can be accomplished. It makes people ask questions. Our presence on the road, in the schools, churches, meetings and in the media disturbed comfortable Canadians and prompted them to seek answers they never previously knew they wanted. There's where opinions can change and pre-conceived notions can also change.

How many people on this campaign said to us "Oh! You mean it's still an issue?" We were having lunch in a restaurant and this one guy, who we hadn't even talked to, walked all the way across the room and rather aggressively leaned over the table "I thought Polio had been wiped out in the 1950s. What's this all about!?"

The disappointing part was finally accepting the reality that we weren't going to meet our fund raising goal. I had originally wanted to raise $10 million, but the board had pared that back to one million dollars. We were almost eighty per cent finished with the cycling trip and all the money raised so far – corporate and government sponsorships, donations, everything – was only about thirty per cent of our target.

I knew that some Rotary clubs sent cheques directly to Polio Plus, with letters attributing the donation to the influence of our campaign, rather than donating to Cycle to Walk – but we had no idea how much that might amount to. Later we found out that there was no way to determine the actual funds contributed. Anything sent to the Canadian head office for Rotary could be tracked but if it was sent directly to Rotary International, other than issuing a receipt, they didn't record where contributions came from and why they were sent.

Out there on the road close to the New Brunswick border, how the fund raising was going was a long way from my mind because I had just been reminded of how hard it was to find a pair of pants I could actually wear.

Just past our last overnight in Quebec, at the small town of Cabano, we ran into some Yukoners. A Whitehorse friend of Doug's, Fred Smith, always says "Live in the Yukon and see the world" because northerners travel a lot. He says it as a joke, but it's true. We encountered them just about everywhere across the country.

These Yukoners, Janice and Rick Jackson, were special for me because Janice works at the place where I get my pants altered. Adjusting my pants isn't just a hemming job, it's almost a work of art. My waist is large because of the size of my upper body. I have one leg that's almost normal sized, for a short person of average waist size. I have one leg that's thinner and shorter than the other one. It was great to see them, especially since I could tell Janice that I didn't need any alterations right now so she didn't have to work.

Then we reached the border and switched flags. There was one flag on the hand cycle and two on the Suburban. Each time we crossed a provincial border, we changed the flags from the province we were finishing to the province we were starting. One of the flags on the Suburban was always the Canadian.

I've always hated putting a flag on a bike. It creates drag on a bike and I like travelling as fast as I can. The first flag we put on in British Columbia was a big orange one, as a safety measure so people in higher vehicles might be able to easier see me. As I plunked my butt into my bike after putting on that first flag, I sliced open three fingers on my left hand when I accidently grabbed the plastic zip tie used to secure it to the pole. That didn't make me like the idea any more than I previously had, but it made sense because it did improve my visibility, so I didn't complain.

Bertha had her birthday party in Grand Falls, New Brunswick – she didn't tell us which birthday it was - at the home of Conrad and Linda Toner. Conrad, who heard about our campaign through Rotary, had never been involved with cycling before nor had he been involved with any cross country fund raiser since Terry Fox. He remembered running into town with Terry and listening to him talk in the town square. When he heard about Cycle to Walk he thought it had been long enough and he should probably be involved in some way.

I was constantly amazed, all the way across the country, at how accommodating Canadians can be. People gave up their rooms, loaned us their homes, made meals and shared so much of themselves so we could feel at home. In our original plan we anticipated the road crew sleeping in the motor home just about every night. Meals were mostly going to be prepared on the motor home stove or a portable barbeque. As the journey progressed, Rotary clubs, churches and communities started providing us with hotel rooms, hosting us at luncheons, breakfasts, barbeques and dinner meetings. People opened up their hearts and their homes.

The farther along we got, as the word spread ahead of us, it just got better. I don't think we spent one night in the motor home from the time we arrived in the Maritimes.

Often after we had left a host billet they would, like the Toners did, drive out on the road just to check on us and say farewell once more. More than once they would turn up at my next presentation in the next town. Once people took it upon themselves to get involved in Cycle to Walk, it seemed difficult to stop it. The entire journey was an experience of people stepping up when we needed them. Canada is a wonderful country, full of wonderful people. It told me that once we, as individuals, decided to do something it could be accomplished.

My hope is that we, as a nation, can send a message to the global community – that we are determined and dedicated to eradicating Polio. And it's the people we met through Cycle to Walk who can accomplish that. Many of them said I inspired them. But in fact, they are the ones who inspired me to believe it truly is possible.

I had never thought of New Brunswick as being a province consisting of hills. When you live in western Canada and think about the Maritimes, we envision fishing villages on rocky, wind swept coastlines, but never think about what's in the interior. Not only do they have hills, they have big hills and long hills. And trees. Forests of them. No windswept rock here. We were all surprised by this.

They have potatoes. I had always heard of "Bud the Spud, from the bright red mud..." but that had been Prince Edward Island. Not until we arrived in Florenceville, the "French Fry Capital of the World", did I really consider New Brunswick to be a major player in the world potato market. Florenceville is the home of Potato World and McCain Foods Ltd., who provided us with accommodations and hosted a luncheon where I gave my presentation. The chairman of the board, Allison McCain, was there with other board members for the presentation. It turned out that not only was he interested in the message but he's a pretty serious bike rider and was very intrigued with the hand cycle.

What I found fascinating was that everything we ate for lunch was made from potatoes. Even the chocolate cake we had for dessert!

Then we went down to the longest covered bridge in the world and I was able to ride across it. It wasn't on the planned route, but it is symbolic of the province and just something I had to do.

Kip Veale joined the road crew in Florenceville. She originally came from the Maritimes but has lived in Whitehorse for years. She and her husband Ron, who is the Supreme Court justice in the Yukon, were friends with my parents when we lived in Whitehorse. It was Kip I called with the Cycle to Walk idea almost four years ago and it was she who told me to talk to Rotary. She didn't pick up rubber bits or sing to Bertha, but she certainly knew a lot of people in the Maritimes. It was nice to have someone, who was there before the beginning, be there with me at the end as well.

The weather bomb hit the road team the day we rode into Saint John. We'd heard so many comments from people about how wet their summer had been, but we'd been lucky so far. We were due for wet weather and we got it!

I almost forgot it was raining when we turned a corner and I caught my first glimpse of the Bay of Fundy. It was then that it hit me, "WOW! We're at the Atlantic Ocean! We're getting close to actually finishing Cycle to Walk!" It didn't seem that long ago that I'd been sitting in a hot tub at the Canada Games Center in Whitehorse thinking about flying down to Victoria and the Pacific Ocean to get started. Time flies when you're having fun!

With eleven speaking engagements scheduled in a single day the road team had one of our busiest non-cycling days of the entire trip. And in between events Chris, working with Kip's son David and his business partner Marilyn Singh who live in Saint John, had scheduled some live radio interviews. We toured City Hall along the way, must have met every Rotarian from the greater Saint John area and ended up spreading the word in the city's largest shopping mall. Even managed to chow down on my first east coast lobster of the trip.

After that schedule, even by non-cycling day standards, my first day back on the hand cycle was a pretty easy one. I rode on the ferry, the Princess of Acadia, in Saint John and rode off a few hours later in Digby, Nova Scotia.

The captain didn't let me pilot this ferry but he did make a public service announcement about us being on board and several people found their way to where we were. One of our visitors was Nova Scotia's Minister of Health, Chris d'Entremont, who had been in Quebec City for meeting of health ministers across Canada. He told us he had already heard of Cycle to Walk at the conference and when he learned we were on board, he just wanted to come and say hello.

This is just one of those odd things that I notice when I'm on the hand cycle. I'm down low enough that I can't see a lot of what people driving cars or trucks can see. I never really know exactly where I am. I often never knew where we started. I was lost during the journey and lost when people ask me where I went.

But I'm low enough that I can see a lot of things they don't. When you spend that much time on a hand cycle every day not even a fully loaded MP3 player can keep you entertained, so you look around and notice stuff. Did you know that in Nova Scotia just about every yard has gnomes or dwarves in it? It must be a cultural thing because I don't remember seeing them anywhere else. It's not something I'm used to seeing. In the Yukon, during summer, people are too busy just trying to get their lawns to grow to decorate them.

I could also see names written on the sides of dog houses. When I spotted 'RAGE' painted on the side of one of them near Shubenacadie, I thought that this might not be one of the better days I've had in my life. The road crew saved me more than once from being turned into a meal for a hungry dog. The small country roads In Nova Scotia are beautiful, but they can be dangerous. The road crew was constantly working to avoid potential threats – like big dogs – or hazardous situations.

It was at Dalhousie University, in Halifax, where we had the kind of presentation I first envisioned when I started to talk about Cycle to Walk. The university has a Global Health Initiative liaison, Alyson Horne-Douma, who pulled together an audience of young adults, medical students, Polio survivors, young parents and one cute little baby. It was a gathering of diverse communities coming together to talk about a forgotten-about disease and what to do about it.

NOVA SCOTIA
PRINCE EDWARD ISLAND

September 6 -21, 2008

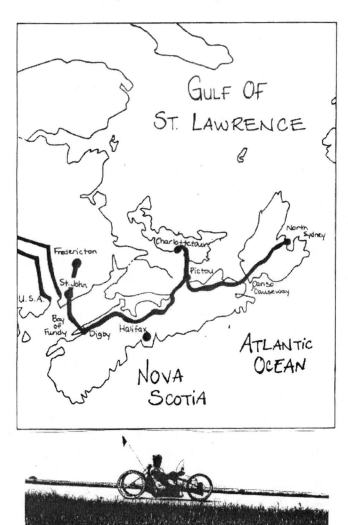

I also had a chance to meet the provincial legislature's Sergeant-At-Arms, Ken Greenham. He's a friend of Rudy and Janet Couture – the people who lived next door to us on Firth Road when I was a kid. Their driveway was one I used to shovel out. Meeting with Ken made me realize how much I owed the Coutures for letting me do that. The work certainly assisted me in developing my upper body strength and that's what had gotten me that far.

After an interview with CTV in Halifax, we were leaving the building when we met a woman named Shauna, who worked in the same building and had Multiple Sclerosis. It turned out she had her own blog site and wrote a very nice piece on it about our meeting.

"I recall reading and hearing about Polio as a young child but it wasn't until the 1980s that I really understood what the disease was all about and the fear it instilled in parents. To this day I don't understand why people don't vaccinate their children against a disease, when the risks of developing the disease are much greater than risk from side effects of the vaccination."

People like Shauna are an inspiration to me. When I last looked at her blog, there was a comment on it about our meeting from a woman in Denver, Colorado. The Cycle to Walk message reaching across an international boundary.

As we approached Pictou, where we caught the ferry to Prince Edward Island, I was reminded of just how long we've been on the road. There were autumn colors along the way and I had to wear warmer clothes. While I was cycling I thought it would nice if there were even more fall colors in the leaves then I took that back when I remembered a simple truth. Fall colors means cooler temperatures.

Prince Edward Island introduced me to a new road hazard. The road side tater. I had never seen so many potatoes on the shoulders of the roads before. Come to think it, I don't think I had ever seen a single potato on the side of any road before. They're not much different than pieces of rubber. I still had to dodge around them. But you can't boil rubber and eat it.

For one of our first meals on PEI, we stopped at a home style restaurant along the highway. I went to the washroom and ran into a few generous bathroom patrons who supported Cycle to Walk. I returned to our table with a handful of donations. For the rest of our meal people stopped by and wished us well or dropped off money. It's exciting when even a trip to the washroom turns into a fund raising event!

I met one of the most inspirational people I have ever encountered. Alex Bain is a marathon runner and a bit of a hero to the people of PEI. In 2006, he ran the entire length of the province to raise awareness about autism and to celebrate ability rather than disability. Alex lives with autism spectrum disorder. Both he and his mother Janet were excited to join me on the cycle into Charlottetown and they had no trouble keeping up.

We had two young girls run out from their driveway to join us for a short distance but they didn't have any shoes on. Their socks were bright red from the mud. They were pretty excited but I don't know if their dad, who was watching from the driveway, was so thrilled. He probably had to wash the socks.

I was asked to make a presentation to the Global Issues class at the University of Prince Edward Island. There were about 60 students there, along with their instructor Barbara Campbell, however the session was taped and, I was told, another 640 students would hear the message via podcast. Although the most effective way to spread a message is through personal contact, it helps to be able to reach out past your physical boundaries and touch people who don't have the opportunity to be there in person.

Even with the limited capabilities that communications had in the first half of last century, the fear of Polio spread at an alarming rate. With today's technology, with information instantly available at your fingertips, it is terrifying to think about how fast a fear like that would be able to spread across the world. Almost as fast as the news that Polio has been eradicated will be communicated to the world!

There is one place in all of Canada that every run, or cycle, or walk across Canada must pass over to complete their journey. If you want to reach or leave Newfoundland, you must cross the Canso Causeway. When you cross the causeway you will meet Rilla and Jim McLean or Yvonne Fox or all three along with various other friends – the "Little Wheels" group. Yvonne started greeting and donating to cross country fund raising journeys on the causeway in 1980 when she was there to greet Terry Fox. Rilla was there for Rick Hansen and the Man in Motion tour in September, 1986. They greeted Dave Shannon when he did his trip in 1997.

We actually missed them on the causeway because we were a day ahead of schedule. So they came out to greet us as we started my second-last day of cycling in Nova Scotia. What a great way to start a day!

Based on a written summary Rilla gave to me this was the third time she had encountered a three wheeled cycle powered by hand. The first time was in 1999. He was a realtor from Whistler, B.C., John Ryan. His tour was called Regeneration Tour. He was riding a 21-speed hand cycle to raise funds for research into spinal cord regeneration.

The second time was in 2001. Stephanie McClellan, suffering from debilitating rheumatoid arthritis and fibromyalgia, who apparently is now a United Church minister in Gander, Newfoundland, completed a cross-country ride she had started in 1999. Her ride, which she called On Wings of Eagles, was to deliver a message that people with disabilities are not just people in need, but people who can contribute and serve their communities in meaningful ways.

Rilla wrote at the bottom of her summary, "I will add Ramesh to my next version of this story."

The next day I cycled until there was no pavement left. Only the sea.

On October 1, 2008, I reached Cape Spear, Newfoundland. Cycle to Walk
ended when I dipped Little Brace in the Atlantic Ocean three times –
once each for education, rehabilitation and education.

The Ever Ascending Path

✦

One thing I will never forget was my last climb out of Petty Harbor, New-foundland, on my last full day of cycling before reaching Cape Spear. It's a traditional Newfoundland fishing community. We had three vehicles that day because Newfoundland Television was filming us and had their own van.

Going four kilometers an hour with a hand cycle and three vehicles through a small coastal community makes a bit of a commotion. People were coming out of their homes to find out what was going on, clapping and cheering. Young people were walking and running alongside of me.

As I was cranking my way up the hill I noticed there was a mother dropping off her son halfway up the hill. She got out of her car and pulled out a bicycle for her son then she drove off and the boy, who was probably about ten or eleven years old, waited for me. When I got to him he hopped on his bike and started riding with me.

We sort-of cycled along in silence because it was uphill and both of us were putting our energy into getting to the top. As we reached the top he looked at me and said "So you're finishing Terry Fox's dream."

I really didn't know what to say. "Yeh. I guess I am. I never really thought about it that way."

"Don't give up," he told me, "You're almost there. I'll be there with you."

He rode a little farther then said "Well, I should get back now, but it was great riding with you." Then he turned around.

That summed up the kind of support I got all along the road. Right from the Yukoners who were behind me from the very beginning almost four years ago to this boy just a few kilometers from the finish.

When we rolled past the 7,000 kilometer mark climbing out of Argentia, Newfoundland, we decided not to do the traditional planting of the marker in the soil beside the highway. We determined to give it to the students at Whitbourne Elementary School when I gave them a presentation the next morning. It seemed so close to the end. There were only a couple of days of cycling left. I opened my presentation by asking the students, "How many know what Polio is?" Not one hand came up. We still have such a long way to go.

I was able to talk to the Sunday school class at Cochrane Street United Church. As I finished up answering questions after my presentation, I overheard a young girl ask her mother if she had received the Polio vaccine when she was young.

When we finished our last full day of cycling, we were just three and a half kilometers from Cape Spear. It was hard to believe that Doug had marked our line on the road for the very last time. It wouldn't be nessecary to mark anything the next time I stop because I would be at our final destination.

A saying I heard on 'The Rock' was "There is no price tag on the doors of Newfoundlanders." That applied right across the country. From everyone we encountered. The outpouring of support – volunteer hours, in-kind donations, meals, billets, sponsors and donations. A material value can't be placed on what Canadians did for Cycle to Walk. And Cycle to Walk is part of the price we must pay for the eradication of Polio.

I looked at the web site for the Global Polio Eradication Initiative the night before we reached Cape Spear and noticed they reported a total of 1,308 new cases in the world so far this year. Children are still dying. They're still getting paralyzed. The real dream was not to reach Cape Spear. The real dream was to educate people and raise funds to help in the eradication of Polio and the restoration of dignity in life for survivors. I can't stop until the World Health Organization has declared this to be a Polio-free world.

John Crosbie, a former Canadian government Minister of Finance, told me at dinner after Cape Spear, "You have not let disability slow you down. What you've done is a great human achievement, and bringing attention back to Polio is an important and noble cause."

There was quite a crowd at Cape Spear. My parents were there. Allon. Geraldine Van Bibber and her husband. Several board members had flown across Canada to be there. Every one was ecstatic to have travelled this far, this long, and to have stayed safe and healthy.

NEWFOUNDLAND

September 22 - October 1, 2008

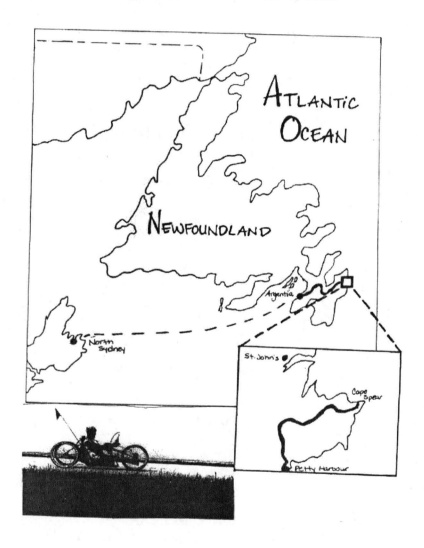

There were so many people around me at Cape Spear it was hard to capture how I felt at that precise moment. I had to think about it for a long time after that day before I fully understood what it meant to me.

I believe everyone deserves respect and dignity and the opportunity to share their gifts with other people. That's what truly made me want to help others around the world. To give others an opportunity to be engaged in their own communities. Not living a life doomed to existing in dirt because of a disease they got because they didn't have access to a couple of drops of vaccination.

I prayed this campaign would give hope and bring attention to the fact that we, as wealthy people in our world, need to take some responsibility and help those who are less fortunate. I think it's the spirit of humanity that we care for one another and that we use medicine to rid the world of disease. I would hope that when we eradicate Polio that we have a successful model that we can use to wipe out other diseases.

The price, if we don't succeed, is that ten million of our children could be paralyzed in the next forty years. I'm not going to drop the ball. I'm not going to give up because I don't want to see anyone in this world living with the effects of a disease that is preventable. Cape Spear was just the start of using my experience with Polio – my life, my disease, the hand cycle, the campaign, the team of people who worked with me - to assist in preventing other cases from occurring anywhere on earth.

I have faith it can work but I believe there needs to be more believers in the world. Through campaigns like Cycle to Walk you educate the public and you develop a wider, more knowledgable base for working together for a Polio-free world.

I think it takes people who have been personally affected by causes to bring attention to diseases. I believe it will work because I need to believe that. I will never lose hope. If I, or people like me, lose hope and stop believing, it will fail. And we will be letting people needlessly suffer. I hope that people will recognize how seriously this is being taken by others and say "Well, how can I get involved? How can I take responsibility and do my part?" Simple. By ensuring your children and grandchildren are vaccinated.

My Dad got onto the extra hand cycle as I got close to Cape Spear and together we rode to the easternmost part of Canada – where my mother waited with "Little Brace". I got one more opportunity to deliver the message, but I'm not sure anyone was listening. They'll say they did but everyone there had heard it umpteen times and some of them had actually written parts of the presentation for me so you can't really blame them if they didn't. I felt it was important to say anyway.

"You need to have a vision," I added, "and goals which inspire you. You need to be passionate about the pursuit of your dreams. We have a responsibility to act and to serve."

Then I took "Little Brace", walked down to the Atlantic Ocean and, like I did in the Pacific Ocean six months earlier, dipped it three times into the surf. Once each for eradication, rehabilitation and education.

Following up on National Immunization Day in Moradabad, India, in November, 2008. Letters and symbols, drawn on the door, identified whether or not the family inside has been immunized and, if not, why not.

Victims of our Own Success

✦

Polio Plus and the Global Polio Eradication Initiative

"I'm not sure exactly what caught my interest," says Doug Ayers about the advent of Rotary International's Polio-Plus program in 1985, "It is such a horrible disease and is so easily prevented. It was one of those targets that seemed so realistic. We could rid the world of Polio. There wasn't any doubt in my mind we could do it.

Then Polio Plus sort of drifted off the front burner for most Rotary clubs in the world. There was a big plan for 20 years (1985-2005), but as it dragged on for ten and fifteen years, people lost interest. Then, when the goal wasn't achieved in 2005, Rotary International added another five years. By the time Ramesh came on the scene, while Rotary International kept Polio Plus alive, the local clubs had moved onto more immediately attainable projects and goals.

Our club, like most local clubs in the world, was doing a minimal effort by 2005. When we did Cycle to Walk we found Rotary Clubs, especially clubs that had been formed after 2000, that had never heard of Polio Plus. We'd respond when Rotary said they needed more money, but that was about it. I know, myself, I thought the job was finished."

Rotary International's campaign to eradicate Polio began in 1979 as a five year project to deliver vaccine to six million children in the Phillipines. The project was successful enough that Rotary decided to take it worldwide.

The guest speaker at the 1985 Rotary International Conference, where Polio Plus was officially launched, was Albert Sabin.

He quoted English admiral Sir Francis Drake "Grant us to know that it is not the beginning but the continuing of the same until it is thoroughly finished that yieldeth the true glory," then added, "I hope you will all dedicate yourself to the true glory – to continue to work until your worthy objectives will be achieved."

Polio Plus made its formal debut in 1986, in India. That year it was a small project in the province of Tamil Nadu. The next year, the program went nationwide with a schedule of vaccinations and surveillance. Between 1991 and 1994, Rotary International organized immunization drives called 'Shishu Suraksha Diwas' (Child Protection Days). By 1994, the government of India had been persuaded of the need for the immunizations and designated two National Immunization Days each year.

In 1988, encouraged by the success of their Expanded Program of Immunization which they started in 1974 and included Polio among the targeted diseases, the World Health Assembly voted to launch the Global Polio Eradication Initiative. The four groups spearheading the initiative were the World Health Organization, (WHO), the United Nations Children's Fund (UNICEF), the U.S. Centers for Disease Control and Prevention (CDC) and Rotary International. The sole purpose was to make Polio the first disease of the 21st century to be eradicated. It was, and still is, the largest public health initiative in world history.

It was a partnership that has proved so successful that former United Nations Secretary General Kofi Annan stated that "Rotary's Polio Plus program is a shining example of the achievements made possible by cooperation between the United Nations and nongovernmental organizations." The four organizations were inducted into the Polio Hall of Fame in Warm Springs, Georgia, in November, 2008.

Polio was endemic in 125 countries on five continents in 1988 and paralyzing more than 1,000 children each day. By 2008, the number of endemic countries shrunk to only four with less than 2,000 cases of Polio reported each year. Approximately two billion children have been immunized. Over 165 million children were immunized in China and India in a single week in 1995.

However, wiping out the last one per cent is proving exceedingly difficult because the majority of the 99 per cent don't realize the one per cent still exists.

"I think we've been partly the victims of our own success," said Allon Reddoch, former president of the Canadian Medical Association and chair of the Cycle to Walk Society, "Because it's ninety-nine per cent gone and people here (in Canada) don't think about India, Pakistan, Afghanistan and Nigeria.

If we could do the same thing with cancer – achieve a 99 per cent reduction in occurance – I daresay there wouldn't be the campaign success the cancer societies have. People would say 'Ninety-nine per cent. Well, that's pretty good. There really isn't a need any more. Let's tackle something else'.

The other problem is that there has been an upswing, in North America in particular, of distrust in immunizations. It doesn't have a scientific basis, but there have been articles linking immunization to catastrophic illnesses. There are some risks for some vaccines. People can actually develop a paralytic Polio from the Sabin vaccine – but Polio cannot be contracted from the inactivated injectible vaccine. In North America it's not much of a problem. As a result, there has been a drift away from vaccines.

If we don't achieve one hundred per cent eradication and people stop immunizing themselves and their children, then it just spreads like any other infectious disease. Once it starts to spread, it has the potential to go around the world."

There are, medical experts agree, five major challenges to eradicating Polio.

1. Halting the exporting of the virus from the remaining endemic countries.

In 2007, there were Polio cases reported in twenty-two countries around the world including the four endemic nations and some countries that hadn't had a case of Polio reported in over 20 years. Most of the cases were isolated and were attributed to travel from endemic countries – but not nessecarily residents of those countries. Some were the result of visits to endemic countries and the virus being transmitted by individuals who lived in Polio-free areas – but who had not been vaccinated against Polio.

2. Halting the spread of the diseases inside the endemic countries.

In 2003, Polio in northern Nigeria had just about been eliminated. There were a few hold-outs who refused but volunteers were approaching them one household at a time and gradually winning them over, convincing them they had a way to stop 'Shan-inna' – the Paralyzing spirit. Then religious zealots got involved.

A physician from the town of Kano, Ibrahm Datti Ahmed, who was also the president of Nigeria's Supreme Council of Sharia Law, started telling people to not take the vaccine because it was free. If it was free, he implied, there had to be something insidious involved, because nothing is free.

Radical clerics took up the call, adding that since the vaccination program was U.S.-backed, there had to be a hidden agenda. The involvement of Rotary, which Muslims in some countries see as a religion in competition with their own, was also used to discourage people from getting immunized. Finally the government imposed an outright ban on vaccinations until it had been tested for other diseases – which many suspected were being passed on secretly to their children along with hormones that would make their daughters infertile.

When the tests were completed and National Immunization Days started again in 2004, with the cooperation of both the government and the clerics, Polio was once again at epidemic proportions. The campaign of suspicion proved to have been more successful than the campaign to restart immunizations. Volunteers were once again forced to move from house to house and slowly, convincing people one at a time – unfortunately not always successfully.

In the eight months that vaccinations in Nigeria were suspended cases in ten west and central African countries, previously deemed to be Polio-free, were attributed to travel by people from northern Nigeria.

When Polio seemed to be on the increase in the Indian state of Uttar Pradesh in 2002, innovative techniques were introduced to overcome resistance. The vaccination teams recruited community religious leaders to their cause because the word of clerics was accepted as the command of God. An announcement, or 'fatwa' from the religious leaders ensured compliance with their wishes. The messages, which told people to disregard the myths and fears of vaccine, were recorded onto audio cassettes and played to the people at their doors.

The results were impressive enough that the program was expanded to other districts where misleading propaganda was creating problems and clerics from many faiths were brought in to assist with the message.

Since 2001, fighting in southern Afghanistan and along the northern Pakistani border has hampered the efforts of volunteers to immunize children. Even a three-day truce, arranged by UNICEF and WHO in June 2008, in southern Afghanistan to permit Polio immunization teams to reach villages isolated by the fighting was violated when Canadian soldiers were attacked near Kandahar City. But violations during the so-called "days of tranquility" are rare. Access Negotiators meet regularly face-to-face with Taliban forces to get permission for health workers to enter into specific areas and arrange for short cease fires during that time.

3. Rapidly stopping Polio outbreaks in previously Polio-free countries.

The east African nation of Somalia was first declared Polio-free in 2002, but in 2005 several hundred cases were reported and the strain of virus was traced back to northern Nigeria. A small army of 10,000 volunteers went to work and immunized almost two million children – including those in the war torn Darfur region. The last case of Polio was reported in March 2007. It takes one year to be considered Polio-free, but it takes three years without a new case before WHO will certify the region as Polio-free.

One of the volunteers in Darfur was a health worker named Ali Mao Moallim. He was the last known person on earth to contract Smallpox, in Somalia in 1977. Smallpox was the first viral disease ever eradicated worldwide in 1979.

4. Addressing the decreasing rate of routine immunizations in Polio-free countries.

Immigrant mothers in Canada apparently have a much better understanding of Polio. According to a study published in Ambulatory Pediatrics in 2008, mothers who have immigrated to Canada – especially those from countries where the effects of contagious diseases is more evident – are more likely to ensure their children are fully immunized than non-immigrant mothers. But, caution the authors of the study, even among the immigrant mothers, "In a system such as Canada's with universal access to all primary care services and high visit rates by children, we have shown that immunization coverage is less than ideal."

There is a full week each year dedicated to raising awareness about the importance of immunization against several diseases. In the United States the CDC spearheads the National Immunization Awareness Week campaign and in Canada it is the Canadian Coalition for Immunization Awareness and Promotion (CCIAP). Resources are provided to local community health centers, health professionals, schools and businesses to set up health fairs, special immunization clinics, school visits and professional education seminars. The program, which was started in 2003, covers 60 countries in the Americas and Africa.

5. Maintaining funding and political commitment.

The amounts of money required are staggering. The cost of the initiative over its 20-year history so far has been approximately four billion dollars with almost $700 million of that amount being raised through Polio Plus. Even with that price tag a Harvard University study in 2007 concluded it would be less expensive in the long run to eradicate Polio than it would be to control and manage the disease.

It has long been accepted that without the support of government the efforts of the initiative would fail. In 2008, Rotary International named German Chancellor Angela Merkel as an Eradication Champion after she convinced the G8 nations to commit to sustaining or increasing contributions to the Global Eradication Initiative. Germany was one of only three G8 countries to increase their contribution in 2007 and was the fourth highest public sector donor. The German government will have contributed $223 million to Polio eradication by the end of 2009. In 2008, Canada increased its contribution from $60 to $90 million.

The Global Alliance for Vaccines and Immunization (GAVI) was founded in 2000 by the Bill & Melinda Gates Foundation, the World Bank, WHO, UNICEF, and vaccine manufacturers. Its objective is to support immunization programs and health systems and accelerate the introduction of new vaccines.

The Bill & Melinda Gates Foundation issued in 2008 a $100 million matching contribution challenge to Rotary International to raise funds for Polio Plus.

The British and German governments joined with Rotary International and the Bill & Melinda Gates Foundation in January, 2009, to inject an additional $630 million.

In addition to money, Rotary clubs from around the world provide a large number of the volunteers who travel to the epicenters of Polio. Many of them are exhilarated and humbled by the magnitude of the challenge.

Wearing baseball caps with "Polio-Plus" printed across the front and yellow vests with Rotary logos and the slogan "Good-bye Polio" written across the back, they walk from door to door in many areas, often being greeted with open arms. Equally often, having to cajole occupants into coming out and allowing their children to receive the two drops or being totally rejected.

The vaccination teams return frequently to the same areas, locating families they missed the first time or trying again with those who refused. Using chalk they mark, on the edge of the door, the date they were at the house and whether or not immunization had taken place. Houses unmarked were probably missed. Doors that had "Rx" marked in chalk beside them were parents who refused, so they try again.

A former Rotary District Governor in Orillia, Ontario, Reid Asselstine, went to India in 2005 and administered vaccine to children. "It's terrific," he said, then added, "This is extremely important. We are so close to completing our mission to eradicate Polio. The last one (Pakistan/Afghanistan) is going to be very expensive because of access to the region. There is a war going on and we are trying to work around that."

For the volunteers, the immunizations can become an affair of the heart which goes beyond protecting children from the virus. Somchai, a 14-year old boy from northern Thailand, was found in 2006 by Polio Plus workers in a thatched hut in that he shared with his mother. Polio had weakened his leg so the foot dropped forward with his toes fixed towards the ground.

The workers contacted a Rotary group called Reaching Overseas with Medical Aid for Children, who arranged for him to be taken to Canberra,

Australia, for surgery in 2008. The group paid for the medical procedure which successfully corrected his foot. Two other Rotarians, David and Akha Stevenson, established a school in his village which Somchai started to attend after returning home.

It is the firm belief of the member organizations of the Global polio Eradication Initiative that if they beat Polio, called by some "the sin of the century", and all that seems to come with it - poverty, prejudice and illiteracy - no goal is beyond their reach and no disease is beyond the capability of medical science to defeat it. It is a battle they feel they can't afford to lose.

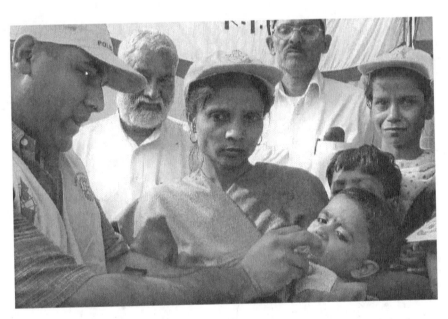

*At the train station on National Immunization Day in Moradabad,
India, in November, 2008. I tentatively administered my
first two drop Polio immunization to a young child.*

Return to India

✦

I was really nervous. I kept thinking 'Two drops only! I can't give this kid four drops. Two drops only!" I didn't know how quickly it came out of the eye dropper. This child was so small and I didn't want to empty the whole thing into his mouth.

When it was done I felt, "Wow! Just two drops! That's unbelievable. Look what I just did. I personally prevented Polio."

In Canada we had been initially disappointed with Rotary International's response to Cycle to Walk. The local Rotary clubs gave us a great reception and they donated time and money to the campaign. Rotary International? Initially they were enthusiastic, then they got into that thing where, if they endorse one project, well there are thousands of other worthy projects out there too and they would have to endorse them all.

What's wrong with endorsing all worthy projects?

As the campaign was winding down in Nova Scotia and Newfoundland, they seemed to decide they wanted to be part of it after all. They assisted us in contacting Rotary clubs and provided some media assistance. Maybe it was the amount of donations that were coming in to Polio Plus with our name on it. Or maybe it was that we had raised the profile of Polio in a lot of communities across Canada. Now, if a Rotary club has a fund raising campaign for Polio Plus they'll have an easier time doing it than they would have earlier. Whatever it was, it was good to have them on board with the campaign at the end.

When I returned to Whitehorse, winter had started to settle in. I was wearing gloves, a toque, my winter jacket and long johns. Then I got a letter from Rotary International asking me if I would be willing to go to India in November to be part of their National Immunization Day.

I jumped at it – as best as I can jump. The chance to defer winter for an extra couple of weeks and help the Polio Plus program was just too much to resist.

When I arrived in Delhi I spent some time at the Indian National Polio Plus Committee office. It was wonderful to be with so many people who work every day and give up so much of themselves for the spirit of humanity and the future of our children. I met Nima Chodon, the center's Communications Associate, my guide and mentor while I was in India.

The next morning we went to the Rotary Institute in Agra, which is in the state of Uttar Pradesh. We spent six hours driving through streets littered with garbage, beggars, wandering cows, cars, buses, motorbikes, cyclists and pedestrians going everywhere. I saw a Polio survivor dragging himself along the ground.

It was a trip that gave me further insight into the mixed blessing that is my life.

If I had received the vaccine, what would my life in india have been? Either way, it looked as if it would have been on the street. Either with no shoes or with bloody knees. If I had received those drops, I probably wouldn't have been a Canadian citizen. With the drops I would have been a healthy part of the world that shunned my mother.

Not getting the drops gave me opportunity, allowed me to escape the poverty, the life on the streets, and enabled me to become their spokesperson.

My first trip, six years earlier, was quite different. I was overwhelmed. It was 'This is the orphanage. This is my birth mother. This is the city I would have been living in.' Whereas, on this trip I looked around more. I saw Polio victims crawling in the dirt. People were more aggressive in begging for money. I saw more poverty. I really got a better sense of the day to day life.

Yet, even with my eyes opened a lot wider than before, I still didn't understand, how could anyone hesitate to receive the Polio vaccine!? It's inexpensive. And available. It prevents a lifetime of suffering.

If you know you haven't received the vaccine and you are even remotely questioning its value, I wish you could see what I saw in India! A young man covered with dirt. He had small, shriveled legs and he crawled on the ground. That is his life. It could have been mine.

Bob Scott, the Chairman of Rotary International's Polio Plus Committee, and his wife Ann were in Agra and we had a short visit. I had met them in Juneau, Alaska, in 2006 when Allon and I attended a Rotary conference there.

The next day we headed to the town of Moradabad, which is where I would participate in National Immunization Day (NID). Again we spent hours dodging buses, cows, cyclists, stray dogs and auto-rickshaws. It was easy to see why Polio is still an issue in India. The water that many of the poor use as a toilet is the same water where they wash themselves or their clothes. Children play there. The environment was so overwhelmingly disturbing for me to accept, yet for millions in India, it is nothing short of normal.

Once in Moradabad, we were given a short orientation about how NID would work. Some areas had been previously identified as high risk – in this district there were 321 high risk areas targeted, of which 208 were in rural settings and 113 in urban. On NID, there were fixed booths in each community, located in the high risk zones. Teams of three, trained vaccinators and supervisors, worked with local volunteers and with medical professionals provided by the Indian government at the booths.

Through the week preceding NID, teams had gone through the community to locate people who hadn't been vaccinated to tell them when and where the booth would be located. This particular year, just over 795,000 homes had been visited.

There were also teams who went to transit points like train stations, bus depots and temporary settlements because many of the people weren't going to come to us, we had to go to them. Nima and I, along with Dr. Mohammad Arif Khan, the field program coordinator for India, were a team at the train station.

It was surreal. I was standing there and someone came over to me and said "They want you to give vaccine to this baby." So over I went. I gave the two drops. That was the first one. There were more, but that first one was the experience of my life. That's a moment I will never forget.

I went to talk at a school later in the afternoon. I was pleased to learn the government requires all schools to be open during NID – even if it falls on a day where school is usually closed. The students are encouraged to be a part of NID by going out to homes and convincing families to bring their children under five to be immunized. Then I met with leaders at the local mosque, part of the Muslim-Ulama Committee which was formed to support Polio eradication efforts, who announced NID from their speakers and encouraged people to go for the vaccinations.

When NID was over, other teams returned to the community for several more days, going from door to door, to find the people who hadn't turned up. Nima, Dr. Khan and I did that job for a few hours the next day then I headed back to Delhi to catch my plane home. I felt proud about what I had done – not just the NID in India, but Cycle to Walk as well. I felt I had taken a part in eradicating Polio which I believe, as long as the resources and efforts continue, can be done within our lifetime.

When you're delivering a message, people listen. They buy into it. They get totally committed to it. Then you're gone and the next speaker comes along. And by the time the next speaker is finished, they've bought into what he or she had to say and have completely forgotten everything you talked about.

So you need to put words into action so they won't forget. That's what Cycle to Walk and going to India for NID was meant to do.

You know what I would like to see and I probably won't be very popular for saying this…

The media is very influential with what the general public believes. It needs to take the message of just how important vaccinations are and put it back in the spotlight.

We talk about the safety of our country. We should not only be getting checked for weapons and explosives when we board an international flight – we should also be asked to provide our immunization records. Before flying anywhere your vaccinations should be up to date. Because it's unfair to the people who could get Polio and be paralyzed by someone who flew in for a business trip or a holiday.

Community leaders need to ensure that public health is top priority and immunizations programs are well advertised and promoted. Not just flu shots or a one time "okay, now we've done it so we can forget about it" shot, but ongoing, annual, regular programs.

School systems need to look at their policies. There needs to be a policy that says, if children aren't vaccinated, this is the risk and this is the outcome. Not a policy that permits exclusion because 'I'm a parent and I, as a parent, don't believe it, or trust it' or 'it's against my religion' - there is no religion on earth that forbids immunization.

I don't think that attitude is realistic or acceptable. There needs to be a policy that says "This is for the safety of every child. No vaccine. No school."

It may go against constitutional rights, but those kinds of rules already exist and are acceptable in society. If a person refuses to let themselves be searched at the airport before boarding a flight, they're not allowed to fly.

I'm reminded every day that this is completely preventable. To know what is possible! It just baffles me that three and a half million Canadians aren't immunized.

I'd like to see the federal government dedicate one cent for every dollar of the Goods and Services Tax collected to the eradication of Polio. Once Polio is gone, to the eradication of the next disease.

We know that Polio is historically the leading cause of disability in the world. We know we have the capability to eradicate it. Taking such a profound step would send a message to Canadians and to the rest of the nations that we're not fooling around. We need to get this done and this is what Canada is going to do to make sure it happens. That way every time someone spends a dollar we're reminded – Polio. We need to eradicate it.

There's an age group that remembers Polio. They had or knew someone who had Polio. Now there are a couple of generations who don't know anyone. Who never felt the fear and dread.

We live in an age of marketing. We need to have clothing companies choose models who are Polio survivors or restricted in their mobility. Pharmaceutical companies who sell their products with the reality of the crawler. By the power of images we can create awareness and education. People, when they see my legs, are educated because now they have a visual of what Polio can do.

Even if we have to do it one hand crank, one person at a time.

After my time with the National Immunization Day team, on the flight to London, England, I sat beside a woman who had just finished adopting a 19-month baby girl from India. I congratulated her on the new addition to her family then asked if her daughter had received the Polio vaccination.

"Yes," she replied with a big smile.

I smiled too.

A "crawler" in Moradabad, India.

"As an international community, we have few opportunities to do something that is unquestionably good for every country and every child, in perpetuity. Polio eradication is one of those opportunities."

Dr. Margaret Chan, Director General, World Health Organization

Chapter Titles

✦

Most chapter titles are taken from inspirational quotations.

Chapter 1: "**Roots of the Past** are deep in the present" unknown (apparently has biblical origins)

Chapter 2: "**The Path to Our Destination** is not always a straight one. We go down the wrong road, we get lost, we turn back. Maybe it doesn't matter which road we embark on. Maybe what matters is that we embark ." Barbara Hall, Northern Exposure, Rosebud, 1993

Chapter 4: "**Where There's a Will**, there's a way" unknown (common)

Chapter 6: "**You Must be the Change** you want to see in the world." Mahatma Ghandi

Chapter 9: "**We Need to be Really Bothered**. How long is it since you were really bothered? About something important, about something real?" Ray Bradbury, Fahrenheit 451

Chapter 12: **Every Great Dream** begins with a dreamer. Always remember, you have within you the strength, the patience, and the passion to reach for the stars to change the world." Harriet Tubman

Chapter 13: "Every day you may make progress. Every step will be fruitful. Yet there will stretch out before you **An** ever-lengthening, **Ever-Ascending**, ever improving **Path**." Sir Winston Churchill

Acknowledgements

✦

My appreciation, not only to those who helped me write this book, but who helped me to write my life. There's not enough room for everyone so if you don't find your name here, I apologize. It doesn't mean I don't appreciate what you have done.

Jan and Ron Ferris. Rani, Matt, Jill, Jenny and Elisa. Doug and Bertha Ayers. Dr. Allon and Mary Reddoch. Sandra Simpson. John Sayer. Chris Madden. Carly Ray. Kip Veale. Lynne Morris. Shelley Williamson. Pixie Ingram. Ivan Zenovitch. Kevin Rumsey. Helene Beaulieu, Carmen Gibbons. Lloyd Axworthy. Val Royle. Mal Malloch. Doug Janzen. Lois Craig. Kate Brent. Bob Lorimer. Audrey McLaughlin. Bonnie Venton Ross. Richard Peter. Marnie Abbott. Pam and Bev Buckway. Dev Hurlburt. James Black. Rod Hill. Chris Simpson. Rev. Dave Pritchard. Geraldine Van Bibber. Chris Rudge. Stephen Burke. Dawn Dimond. Cheryl Smith. Patricia Halladay. Joy Wickett, Allain Dallaire, Sandy Coleman.

The Government of Yukon. Rotary Clubs across Canada. Rotary International's Polio Plus. Sanofi-Pasteur. Dr. Chris Rutty. Anglican and United Churches across Canada. 'A Touch of Class' – Barry Kitchen and friends. Larry Bagnall. My dieticians: Laura Wilson, Lisa Vowk and Donna Carrigan. Cathy Foster. Alex Furlong and the Yukon Federation of Labour. Andrea Rodgers at Sportees. Adam Green at Terra Firma. Northern Visions Development. McCain's. Norcan. Confederation College. Air North. All Weather Windows. Optometrists Building, Rev. Mary Battija, Nancy Ringham, Joel Macht.Tim Frick. Sue Meikle. Julie Robinson. France Robert. Leilah Cross. Daniel Dunfy. Darla, Cress and Taliah Lundstrom. Rev. Sean Murphy. Bishop Terry Buckle. Madeline and Simon Piuze. Sarah Walls. Jennifer Scott.

Jon Breen. Cherylee Morrison. Carol Corbet. Tim Brady. Stephen Reid.

Matt Poushinsky. Jody Studney. Kevin Mellis. Mireille Simon. Tim Ng. Sara Galbraith. Nikki Staszewski. Elizabeth Soloway. Sara Pyke.

Lotteries Yukon and the Yukon Government's Advanced Artists program.

Rick Hansen. Terry Fox – for your inspiration.

And , last but not least. My biological mother, Lakshmi. Your courage gave me my life.

Bibliography

✦

Newspapers/Magazines/radio/televison

Yukon News, Whitehorse Star, Metro Halifax, Metro Toronto, The Sault Star, The Rotarian, Halifax Herald, Regina Leader-Post, Canadian Broadcasting Corporation (CBC), Pittsburgh Post-Gazette (USA), The Statesman (India), Canberra Times (Australia), Canadian Press, New York Times (USA), BBC News (England), Newman Times-Herald (USA), Halifax Chronicle-Herald, Woodstock Bugle-Observer, Fredricton Daily Gleaner, CTV, Peterborough Examiner, Toronto Sun, Owen Sound Sun Times, Thunder Bay Chronicle Journal, Kenora Daily Miner & News, Elliot Lake Standard, SooNews, Toronto Globe and Mail, Quebec City Chronicle-Telegraph, Kamloops Daily News, Anglican Journal, Regina Leader-Post, Brandon Sun, Winnipeg Free Press, New York Daily News (USA), Harvard University Gazette (USA), Conntact, Toronto Star, San Francisco Chronicle (USA), Associated Press (USA), Upper Ottawa Valley Daily Observer, American Journal of Public Health (USA), Washington Post (USA), New York Herald Tribune (USA), New Zealand Herald (New Zealand), Medical Journal of Australia (Australia), Vancouver Province, Edmonton Journal

Books/Papers

Polio: An American Story, David M. Oshinsky, Oxford University Press, 2004

The History of Polio, Christopher J. Rutty, Health Heritage Research Services (originally prepared for Sanofi-Pasteur in 2002)

Conquering the Crippler, Canada and the Eradication of Polio, Christopher J. Rutty, Canadian Journal of Public Health, 2005

Small Wheels Across the Causeway, Rilla McLean, unpublished

Springtime in the Rockies, Bertha Ayers, unpublished

Cycle to Walk Journals 1 to 3, Bertha Ayers , unpublished

The Angels in Our Path, Bertha Ayers, unpublished

Serologic Epidemiology of Poliomyelitis, Joseph Melnick, John Paul, Mary Walton, 1954

Breaking the Back of Polio, David M. Oshinsky, Yale Medicine, 2005

The Twentieth Century Plague, Christopher J. Rutty

Internet

Wikipedia, Cycle to Walk, Rotary International News, The Packet and Times, NovaNewsnow, Run for 1 Planet, Giddy Up for Wishes, Wheel to Walk, News-Medical.net, Pharmaceutical Business Review, Newswith-views.com

Other

National Center for Immunization and Respiratory Diseases, Centers for Disease Control and Prevention National Immunization Program (CDC), Global Polio Eradication Initiative, Canadian International Immuniza-tion Initiative, UNICEF, The Rotary Foundation, Multifaith Walk Against Violence, The Nobel Foundation, Academy of Achievement, Cincinnati Children's Hospital, National Polio Survivors Network, March of Dimes, Women in History, World Health Organization, Minnesota Department of Health, Families for Children

The Authors

✦

As a result of completing Cycle to Walk Ramesh Ferris was nominated for the 2008 Ontario Premiers Award for Graduates of Ontario Colleges of Applied Arts and Technology and as Volunteer of the Year for the City of Whitehorse, Yukon. He received the 2009 Yukon Tourism Championship Award from the Government of the Yukon, was selected as an honorary torch bearer for the Olympic Games to be held in Vancouver, B.C., in 2010 and presented with a Paul Harris Fellowship from the Rendezvous Rotary Club of Whitehorse. After joining the Rotary Club in Whitehorse he was named chair of their PolioPlus committee. He is in the process of establishing the Ramesh Ferris Foundation to assist in the battle to eradicate Polio. You can find more information on his website at *RAMESHFERRIS.COM*.

John Firth was born in Edmonton, Alberta, and adopted into the Yukon Territory. Growing up in Whitehorse and Dawson City he worked as a journalist, prospector, public relations director, theatre owner, financial advisor and is now a professional full time writer. He makes his home in Whitehorse where he is the chair of Yukon Foundation. In 1997 he received the Commissioners Award for Public Service for his work in preserving Yukon history and culture. He sits on the editorial advisory board for Up Here Business Magazine and is the author of two previous books, Yukon Quest (Lost Moose Publishing, 1998) and River Time (Newest Publishing, 2004). You can find more information on his website at *johnfirth.ca*